IDIOT'S DELIGHT

BY

ROBERT E. SHERWOOD

★

DRAMATISTS
PLAY SERVICE
INC.

This play is lovingly dedicated to
Lynn Fontanne
and
Alfred Lunt

IDIOT'S DELIGHT was presented by the Theatre Guild at the National Theatre, Washington, D.C., on March 9, 1936. The set design was by Lee Simonson. The following cast:

DUMPTSY	George Meader
ORCHESTRA LEADER	Stephen Sandes
DONALD NAVADEL	Barry Thompson
PITTALUGA	S. Thomas Gomez
AUGUSTE	Edgar Barrier
CAPTAIN LOCICERO	Edward Raquello
DR. WALDERSEE	Sydney Greenstreet
MR. CHERRY	Bretaigne Windust
MRS. CHERRY	Jean Macintyre
HARRY VAN	Alfred Lunt
SHIRLEY	Jacqueline Paige
BEULAH	Connie Crowell
BEBE	Ruth Timmons
FRANCINE	Etna Ross
ELAINE	Marjorie Baglin
EDNA	Frances Foley
MAJOR	George Greenberg
FIRST OFFICER	Alan Hewitt
SECOND OFFICER	Winston Ross
THIRD OFFICER	Gilmore Bush
FOURTH OFFICER	Tomasso Tittoni
QUILLERY	Richard Whorf
SIGNOR ROSSI	LeRoi Operti
SIGNORA ROSSI	Ernestine de Becker
MAID	Una Val
ACHILLE WEBER	Francis Compton
IRENE	Lynn Fontanne

ACT ONE

Afternoon of a winter day in any imminent year.

ACT TWO

Scene 1 — Eight o'clock that evening.
Scene 2 — Eleven o'clock that evening.
Scene 3 — After midnight.

ACT THREE

The following afternoon.

CHARACTERS

Dumptsy
Orchestra Leader
Donald Navadel
Pittaluga
Auguste
Captain Locicero
Dr. Waldersee
Mr. Cherry
Mrs. Cherry
Harry Van
Shirley
Beulah
Bebe
Francine
Elaine
Edna
Major
First Officer
Second Officer
Third Officer
Fourth Officer
Quillery
Signor Rossi
Signora Rossi
Anna
Achille Weber
Irene

The scene of the play is the cocktail lounge in the Hotel Monte Gabriele, in the Italian Alps, near the frontiers of Switzerland and Austria.

IDIOT'S DELIGHT

ACT ONE

Scene: The modernistic cocktail lounge of the Hotel Monte Gabriele. The hotel is a small one, which would like to consider itself a first class resort. Its Italian management (this was formerly Austrian territory) has refurnished it, added this cocktail lounge and a few modern bedrooms with baths, in the hope that some day Monte Gabriele may become a rival for St. Moritz. So far, this is still a hope. Although the weather is fine, the supply of winter sports enthusiasts at Monte Gabriele is negligible, and the hotel is relying for its trade upon those itinerants who, because of the current political situation, are desirous of leaving Italy. Near at hand are a railway line into Switzerland, highways into Switzerland and Austria, and an Italian army airport. When people make their exits and entrances through the arch center, if they go or come in from the outside they enter from left of arch and when going into the interior of the hotel they go right of arch. At the left, up-stage center, is a large doorway, leading to the lobby. At lower right is a staircase. A few steps up is a landing, above which are three large windows with a fine view of the Alpine scenery to the north and west. There is a Venetian blind on each window. They are rolled up at the moment. From the landing the stairs continue up to a gallery which leads to bedrooms off to the upper left. Down left is a swinging door marked above with the word "BAR." Above that is another door over which is marked "SALONE." This door is never used in the action. Up center is a long, modernistic built-in leather seat. In front of the seat are two small, round modernistic tables. They are spaced about four feet apart. There is another similar seat, but smaller, down left, below bar door. It, too, has a small table in front of it. Another table down right with chair above it.

Another table up in left upstage corner, above piano with a chair above table. Also a table in corner of where seat up center goes up vertically. A slightly larger, round table, but of the same design and color, stands down left below piano. It has an armchair left of it, a side chair above it and a side chair right of it. There are handbells and ashtrays and matches on each table. At left above entrance to bar is a platform, on which is a modernistic piano. There is a piano bench above piano. Left of piano, on platform, are two chairs, one for the saxophonist and the other for the drummer, who also has his drum, etc. left of piano and downstage, and when first curtain rises a dismal little four-piece orchestra is playing.

Note: A line of the dialogue along toward the end of Act One: "there is something about this place that suggests a vague kind of horror." This is nothing definite, or identifiable, or even immediately apparent. Just an intimation.

Pittaluga is the owner and manager of the hotel. He is a fussy, worried Italian in the conventional morning coat and striped pants. Stretched out on seat up center, looking dolefully out window, is Donald Navadel, a rather precious, youngish American, suitably costumed for winter sports by Saks Fifth Avenue. Experienced in the resort business, he was imported this year to organize sporting and social life at Monte Gabriele with a view to making it a Mecca for American tourists. He is not pleased with the way things have turned out. Dumptsy stands up center between seat up center and piano platform. He is a humble, gentle little bellboy, aged about forty, born in this district when it was part of Austria, but now a subject of the Fascist Empire. He has been cleaning ashtrays. He listens to music. (The name is pronounced "DOOM-PTSY.") The employees of the hotel and the Italian officers converse with each other in Italian. There are also a few words of German here and there.

DUMPTSY. *(U.C.R. of musicians' platform.) Come si chiama questa musica che suonate?*

ORCHESTRA LEADER. *"Giugno in Gennaio."*

DUMPTSY. *Oh, com'e bello! Mi piace! (Turns R. to Don.)* It's good.

DON. *(Seated on seat U.R.C. His patience is exhausted.)* Will you please for God's sake stop playing that same damned tiresome thing?

DUMPTSY. You don't like it, Mr. Navadel? *(Speaks English with a slight German accent.)*

DON. I'm so sick of it I could scream!

DUMPTSY. I like it. To me it's good.

DON. Go on, and clean the ashtrays.

DUMPTSY. *(Crosses R. to table below Don.)* But they're not dirty, sir. Because there's nobody using them.

DON. There's no need to remind me of *that!* Do as you're told!

DUMPTSY. If you please, sir. *(Picks up ashtray, blows on it — whistles tune, goes U.C., exits through arch and L.)*

DON. *(To Leader.)* You've played enough. Get out!

PALETA. Is not yet three o'clock.

DON. Never mind what time it is. *(Orchestra stops playing.)* There's nobody here to listen to you. So you can just save the wear and tear on your harpsichord and go grab yourselves a smoke.

PALETA. Very good, Mr. Navadel. *(To other musicians.)* E'Inutile suonare piu. Non ascolta. No, Andiamo e fumar una sigarette. *(They put away instruments and music and start U.C. as Pittaluga, bristling, enters R. from arch U.C.)*

PITTALUGA. *(To Paleta, the pianist.)* Eh, professori? Per che avete fermato di suonari? Non sono ancora le tre.

PALETA. Domanda il Signor Navadel. *(Exits through arch U.C. and L., followed by musicians.)*

PITTALUGA. *(Comes D.L. of Don.)* You told my orchestra it could stop? *(He speaks English with marked Italian accent.)*

DON. *(Untroubled.)* I did.

PITTALUGA. My orders to them are they play in here until three o'clock. Why do you take it to yourself to countermand my orders?

DON. Because their performance was just a little too macabre to be bearable.

9

PITTALUGA. *(Furious.)* So! You have made yourself the manager of this hotel, have you? You give orders to the musicians. Next you will be giving orders to me — and to the guests themselves, I have no doubt ... *(Crosses L. to table D.L. and rearranges ashtray and bell on table.)*

DON. The guests! *(Laughs dryly, sits up.)* That's really very funny. Consult your room chart, my dear Signor Pittaluga, and let me know how many guests there are that I can give orders to. The number when last I counted was three.

PITTALUGA. *(Crosses R. and U.L. of Don.)* And you stop being insolent, you — *animale fetente*. I pay you my money, when I am plunging myself into bankruptcy ...

DON. Yes, yes — we know all about that. You pay me your money. And you have a perfect right to know that I'm fed to the teeth with this little pension that you euphemistically call a high-grade resort hotel. Indeed, I'm fed to the teeth with you personally.

PITTALUGA. *(In a much friendlier tone.)* Ah! So you wish to leave us! I'm very sorry, my dear Donald. We shall miss you.

DON. My contract expires on March the first. I shall bear it until then. *(Lies down, fully stretched out on seat.)*

PITTALUGA. You insult me by saying you are fed with me, but you go on taking my money?

DON. *(Yawning.)* Yes!

PITTALUGA. *(Sits L. of Don on seat U.C.)* Mascalzone di prima sfera prepotente, farabutto, canaglia ...

DON. And it's not going to do you any good to call me names in your native tongue. I've had a conspicuously successful career in the resort hotel business, all the way from Santa Barbara to St. Moritz. And you lured me away from a superb job ... with your glowing descriptions of this place, crowds of sport lovers, desperately chic — *(Pittaluga rises, crosses R. below Don, faces him.)* flocking here from London, Paris, New York ...

PITTALUGA. Did *I* know what was going to happen? Am *I* the king of Europe?

DON. You are the proprietor of this obscure tavern, and you're responsible for the fact that it's a deadly, boring dump!

PITTALUGA. Yes! And I engaged you because I thought you

10

had friends — rich friends ... and they would come here after you instead of St. Moritz, and Muerren, and Chamonix. And where are your friends? What am I paying you for? To countermand my orders and tell me you are fed ... *(Wails from warning sirens are heard off R.) Che succede?*

DON. *(Sits up quickly.)* That's from down on the flying fields.

PITTALUGA. It is the warning for the air raids. *(Don rises, crosses R. to window, followed by Pittaluga. Auguste, the barman, is heard in bar off L.)*

AUGUSTE. *(Off.) Vas is los? (Comes in from bar L., stands at below piano.) Che cosa?*

PITTALUGA. *(L. of Don, looking through window.) Segnali D'incursiene. La guerra e incomminiciata e il nemico viene. (Airplane motors heard off R.)*

DON. *(Looking through window.)* Look! The planes are taking off. They're the little ones — the combat planes. *(Captain Locicero enters from L. and arch C. He is the officer in charge of the frontier station. He is tired, quiet, nice. He comes D. to above table D.L. Dumptsy follows Captain on through arch U.C.)*

AUGUSTE. *Signor Capitano!*

CAPTAIN. *Buona sera! (Auguste helps him take off his cape and Captain gives him his hat.)*

DUMPTSY. *(R. of Captain.) Cosa succede, Signor Capitano? E la guerra?*

CAPTAIN. No — no — *datemi un cognac e soda. (Takes off gloves and puts them and riding crop on table D.L. Auguste gives Captain's cape and hat to Dumptsy and exits into bar L. Dumptsy puts cape and hat on seat L. of table, goes U. and exits through arch C. Captain sits chair L. of table, takes a cigarette case from pocket of his tunic as Pittaluga crosses to Captain. Don follows to R. of Pittaluga.)*

AUGUSTE. *(As he goes out.) Si, Signor.*

PITTALUGA. *Cosa significano quei terribli segnali? E il nemico che arriva, forse?*

DON. What's happened, Captain? Is there an air raid? Has war started?

CAPTAIN. *(Speaks English with a Continental accent, but it would be difficult to say of what country he is a native. Smiling.)* Who knows? But there is no air raid. They're only testing the sirens,

11

to see how fast the combat *(Handbell is heard, off U.C.)* planes can go into action. You understand — it's like lifeboat drill on a ship. *(Lights cigarette. Dumptsy enters L. through arch C.)*

DUMPTSY. 'Scuse, padrone. *Due Inglesi arrivati. (Exits hurriedly through arch C. and L. Don goes to seat U.C.)*

PITTALUGA. *Vengo subito. 'Scusa, Signor Capitano. (Exits hurriedly through arch C. and L.)*

CAPTAIN. Have a drink, Mr. Navadel?

DON. *(Puts on skiing jacket.)* Forgive me, Captain — but two guests are actually arriving. I must go out and be affable. *(Exits through arch C. and L. Dr. Waldersee appears on gallery above with a book in his hand, and pauses on stairs as Auguste enters from bar L. and serves Captain with brandy and soda, and exits into bar. Doctor is an elderly, stout, crotchety, sad German.)*

CAPTAIN. Good afternoon, Doctor. Have a drink?

DOCTOR. Thank you very much — no. What is all that aeroplanes? *(Speaks English with a German accent.)*

CAPTAIN. This is a crucial spot, Dr. Waldersee. We must be prepared for visits from the enemy.

DOCTOR. Enemy, eh? And who is that?

CAPTAIN. I don't quite know, yet. The map of Europe supplies us with a wide choice of opponents. I suppose, in due time, our government will announce its selection — and we shall know just whom we are to shoot at.

DOCTOR. *(Starts coming downstairs.)* Nonsense! Obscene nonsense.

CAPTAIN. Yes — yes. But the taste for obscenity is incurable, isn't it? *(Takes sip of his brandy and soda.)*

DOCTOR. *(Stops on middle landing.)* When will you let me go into Switzerland?

CAPTAIN. Again I am powerless to answer you. My orders are that no one for the time being shall cross the frontiers, either into Switzerland or Austria.

DOCTOR. And when will this "time being" end?

CAPTAIN. When Rome makes its decision between friend and foe.

DOCTOR. I am a German subject. I am not your foe.

CAPTAIN. I am sure of that, Dr. Waltersee. The two great Fascist states stand together, against the world.

DOCTOR. *(Passionately.)* Fascism has nothing to do with it! I am a scientist. I am a servant of the whole damn stupid human race. *(Comes down rest of stairs.)* If you delay me any longer here, my experiments will be ruined. *(Puts book on table below L. end of seat U.C., crosses L. to Captain.)* Can't you appreciate that? I must get my rats at once to the laboratory in Zurich, or all my months and years of research will have gone for nothing. *(Don enters L. and arch C. followed by Mr. and Mrs. Cherry, a pleasant young English couple in the first flush of their honeymoon. Doctor goes U. to seat U.C. and sits R. end of it.)*

DON. And this is our cocktail lounge. *(Crosses L. below piano, points to bar.)* Here is the American bar. We have a *thé dansant* here every afternoon at 4:30 and supper dancing in the evening.

CHERRY. *(L. of Mrs. Cherry, holding her hand.)* Oh, it's charming!

DON. Your rooms are up there, opening off that gallery. All this part of the hotel is quite new. *(Crosses R. below Mr. and Mrs. Cherry to window.)* I think you'll concede that the view from here is absolutely unparalleled. From here we can look into four countries. *(Dumptsy crosses from L. to R. at back with Cherry's suitcases. Captain takes out notebook and pencil from breast pocket and jots down some notes. Doctor reads his book.)* Here in the foreground, of course, is Italy. This was formerly Austrian territory, transferred by the Treaty of Versailles. *(The Cherrys come D. and cross R.)* It's called Monte Gabriele in honor of D'Annunzio, Italian poet and patriot. Over there is Austria — and over there is Switzerland. *(The Cherrys go U. two steps and look through window, backs to audience.)* And far off, you can just see the top of a mountain peak which is in the Bavarian Tyrol. Rather gorgeous, isn't it?

CHERRY. *(L. of Don.)* Yes.

MRS. CHERRY. *(L. of Cherry.)* Darling — *look* at that sky!

CHERRY. I say! It is good.

DON. Do you go in for winter sports, Mrs. Cherry?

13

MRS. CHERRY. Oh, yes — I — my husband and I are very keen on them. *(Pittaluga from L. and Dumptsy from R. appear in arch C. They speak in Italian through following dialogue onstage. Quillery crosses from L. to R. at back, above Pittaluga and Dumptsy. He is wearing hat and overcoat.)*

PITTALUGA. Dumptsy!
DUMPTSY. *Si, Padrone?*   *(Pittaluga*
PITTALUGA. *E il bagaglio e portato su?*   *and Dumptsy*
DUMPTSY. *Gia sopra. Portato su. Portato su.*   *speak at the*
PITTALUGA. *Sta bene va fare, va fare.*   *same time as*
(Comes D., crosses R. to stairs.)   *Don and*
DON. Splendid! We have everything here.   *Cherry.)*
CHERRY. I've usually gone to Kitzbuhel.

DON. It's lovely there, too.
CHERRY. But I hear it has become much too crowded there now. I — my wife and I hoped it would be quieter here.
DON. Well — at the moment — it is rather quiet here.
PITTALUGA. *(At foot of stairs. To Cherry.)* Your luggage has been sent up, Signor. Would you care to look at your rooms now?
CHERRY. Yes, thank you.
PITTALUGA. If you will have the goodness to step this way. *(Goes upstairs.)*
CHERRY. *(Pauses at window on way U. with Mrs. Cherry.)* What's that big bare patch down there?
DON. *(Casually.)* Oh, that's the airport. *(Pittaluga coughs discreetly.)* We have a great deal of flying here.
PITTALUGA. Right this way, please.
CHERRY. Oh — I see. *(They continue on U., preceded by Pittaluga.)*
DON. And you will come down for the *thé dansant?*
MRS. CHERRY. We should love to.
DON. Splendid!
PITTALUGA. *(Stops at L. of doorway and they pass him.)* Right straight ahead, please. *No no per piacere! Non quella la stanza un*

14

apartamento nuziale! (They exit through gallery.)
DON.   *(Standing on first step.)* Honeymooners.
CAPTAIN.   *(Puts notebook and pencil in breast pocket.)* Yes — poor creatures.
DON.   They wanted quiet.
DOCTOR.   When will you know when I can go into Switzerland?
CAPTAIN.   The instant that word comes through from Rome, Dr. Waldersee. *(Handbell is heard, off U.C.)* You must understand that I am only an obscure frontier official. And here in Italy, as in your own Germany, authority is centralized.
DOCTOR.   *(Rises, crosses L. To Captain.)* But you can send a telegram to Rome, explaining the urgency of my position.
DUMPTSY.   *(Appears in arch C. from L. and comes D. greatly excited.)* Mr. Navadel!
DON.   Yes?
DUMPTSY.   More guests from the bus, Mr. Navadel. Seven of them! *(Exits arch C. and L.)*
DON.   Seven! *Good* God! *(Crosses hurriedly L. and U. and exits through arch C. and L.)*
DOCTOR.   *Ach, es hat keine ruhe hier.*
CAPTAIN.   I assure you, Dr. Waldersee, I shall do all in my power.
DOCTOR.   *(Sits chair R. of table D.L. opposite Captain.)* They must be made to understand that time is of vital importance.
CAPTAIN.   Yes, yes. Of course.
DOCTOR.   I have no equipment here to examine them properly — no assistant for the constant observation that is essential if my experiments are to succeed ...
CAPTAIN.   *(A trifle wearily.)* I'm so sorry ...
DOCTOR.   *Ja!* You say you are so sorry. But what do you *do?* You have no comprehension of what is at stake. You are a soldier and indifferent to death. You say you are so sorry, but it is nothing to you that hundreds of thousands, *millions,* are dying from a disease that is within my power to cure!
CAPTAIN.   Again, I assure you, Dr. Waldersee —
DON.   *(Heard offstage in arch U.C.)* Our Mr. Pittaluga will be

15

down in a moment. In the meantime, perhaps you and — the others ... (*Enters from L. through arch C., followed by Harry Van, a lean, thoughtful, lonely American vaudeville manager, promoter, press agent, book agent, crooner, hoofer, barker or shill. He has undertaken all sorts of jobs in his time, all of them capitalizing his powers of salesmanship, and none of them entirely honest. He wears a snappy, belted polo coat and a brown felt hat with brim turned down on all sides and carries briefcase under his arm.*) would care to wait in here. This is the cocktail lounge. We have a *thé dansant* here every afternoon at 4:30 and supper dancing in the evening ... (*They come D.C. and R. of Doctor, as Doctor lights cigar and Captain takes drink.*)

HARRY. (*L. of Don. Takes hat off.*) Do you run this hotel?

DON. No. I'm the social manager.

HARRY. The what?

DON. The social manager.

HARRY. You're an American, aren't you?

DON. I am. Santa Barbara's my home, and Donald Navadel is my name.

HARRY. Glad to know you. My name's Harry Van. (*They shake hands.*)

DON. Glad to know you, Mr. Van. Are you — staying with us long?

DOCTOR. (*Rises, to Captain.*) I will myself send a telegram to Rome, to the German Embassy. (*Goes U. and exits through arch C. and L.*)

CAPTAIN. They might well be able to expedite matters.

HARRY. (*Speaks to Don through two foregoing speeches.*) Well, I don't know. Maybe you can help me out?

DON. I'm here to be of service, in any way I can. (*Dumptsy crosses from L. to R. at back with Harry's Gladstone bag.*)

HARRY. I've got to get over that border. When I came in on the train from Fiume, they told me the border is closed, and maybe the train is stuck here for tonight or maybe longer. When I asked them why, they either didn't know or they refused to divulge their secret to me. What seems to be the trouble? (*Captain finishes drink and puts out cigarette during Harry's speech.*)

DON. Perhaps Captain Locicero can help you. He's the commander of Italian headquarters here. This is Mr. Van, Captain.

CAPTAIN. *(Rising.)* Mr. Van, my compliments. *(They shake hands over table.)*

HARRY. And mine to you, Captain. I'm trying to get to Geneva.

CAPTAIN. You have an American passport?

HARRY. I have. Several of them. *(Reaches in his pocket, takes out seven passports. He fans them like a deck of cards and hands them to Captain.)*

CAPTAIN. You have your family with you?

HARRY. Well — it isn't exactly a family. *(Goes to the R.)* Come on in here, girls!

SHIRLEY. *(Off.)* OK, Harry. Come on in, kids. Harry wants us. *(Six chorus girls come in. They are wearing winter coats, hats, furs and galoshes and carry their hand luggage, umbrellas, etc. They are named and enter in following order: Shirley, Edna, Beulah, Bebe, Francine, and Elaine. Shirley, Beulah, and Bebe come D. to seat C. and Beulah sits at L. end of seat C. Shirley stands R. of Beulah. Edna stands R. of piano, Francine stands R. of Edna and Elaine stands R. of Edna. Of these, Shirley is the principal, a frank, knowing dancer. Beulah is a bubble dancer. Bebe is a hard, dumb little number who shimmies. The other three don't much matter. Don doesn't know quite how to take the surprising troupe, but Captain is impressed, favorably.)*

HARRY. Captain, allow me to introduce the girls. We call them "Les Blondes." We've been playing the Balkan circuit — Budapest, Bucharest, Sofia, Belgrade, Zagreb — *(Turns to Don.)* Back home, that would be the equivalent to "Pan Time."

CAPTAIN. *(Bowing.)* How do you do?

GIRLS. How do you do ... Pleased to meet you ... *(Etc.)*

HARRY. *(Crosses L.)* The situation in brief is this, Captain. We've got some very attractive bookings at a night spot in Geneva.

CAPTAIN. Um — h'm?

HARRY. Undoubtedly the League of Nations feel that they need us. Ha-ha. It's important that we get there at once. So, I'd be grateful for prompt action.

CAPTAIN. *(Looking at first passport.)* Miss Shirley — Laughlin.

HARRY. *(Crosses R.)* Laughlin. This is Shirley. Step up, honey. *(Shirley steps forward and crosses L. to Captain.)*

CAPTAIN. *(Pleased with Shirley.)* How do you do?

SHIRLEY. How do you do?

CAPTAIN. This photograph hardly does you justice.

SHIRLEY. *(Comes D. to Captain.)* I know. It's terrible, isn't it!

HARRY. *(Interrupting Shirley's obvious flirtation by snapping his fingers.)* Who's next, Captain? *(Shirley goes U. to below piano.)*

CAPTAIN. Miss Beulah Tremoyne.

HARRY. Come on, Beulah. *(She rises — comes forward in a wide sweep, as she crosses L.)* Beulah is our bubble dancer. She's the product of the esthetic school, and therefore more of a dreamer.

CAPTAIN. *(Laughs.)* Ho, ho, ho! Exquisite!

BEULAH. *(About to sit on chair R. of table D.L.)* Thank you *ever* so much.

HARRY. That'll be all, Beulah. *(Beulah crosses R., sits L. end of seat C.)* Who's next, Captain?

CAPTAIN. *(Reading off names from passports.)* Miss Elaine Messiger!

HARRY. Elaine! *(Elaine takes off hat, shakes her hair.)*

CAPTAIN. Miss Francine Merle!

HARRY. La Flame!

CAPTAIN. Miss Edna Creesh!

EDNA. H'y'a!

HARRY. *(To Edna, under his breath.)* Turn off the engine.

CAPTAIN. And Miss Bebe Gould!

HARRY. You'll find Bebe a very lovely little girl.

BEBE. *(Remonstratively.)* Ha-rry!

HARRY. Come on, honey! *(Bebe comes D., stands below Beulah and L. of Harry.)* Bebe is our shimmy artiste, but incorrigibly unsophisticated! *(Bebe saucily tosses her head at Harry and goes U. to seat C.)*

CAPTAIN. Very beautiful. Very, very beautiful!

SHIRLEY. Thank you! *(Crosses R., below group to C. of seat U.C.)*

CAPTAIN. Mr. Van, I congratulate you.

HARRY. *(Crosses L. to Captain.)* And now can we —

CAPTAIN. And I wish that I, too, were going to Geneva. *(Hands passports back to Harry.)*

HARRY. Then it's OK for us to pass?

CAPTAIN. But won't you young ladies sit down?

SHIRLEY. Thanks, Captain. *(Sits C. of seat U.C. Bebe sits L. of Shirley, Elaine L. of Beulah.)*

EDNA. We'd love to. *(Sits on suitcase R. of piano.)*

FRANCINE. I'll say. *(Goes U., sits on piano bench and lights cigarette. Beulah, feeling at home, takes off shoes.)*

(Spoken together.)

HARRY. Listen, Captain, I don't want to seem oblivious to your courtesy, but the fact is we can't afford to hang around here any longer. That train may pull out and leave us.

CAPTAIN. I give you my word that train will not move tonight, and maybe not tomorrow night, and maybe never. *(Bows deeply.)* It is a matter of the deepest personal regret to me, Mr. Van, but —

HARRY. Listen, pal. Just stop being polite for a minute, will you? And tell me how do we get to Geneva.

CAPTAIN. *(Crosses to seat D.L., picks up cape and hat.)* That is not for me to say. I am as powerless as you are, Mr. Van. I, too, am a pawn. *(Crosses R. above Harry and U.C.)* But, speaking for myself, I shall not be sorry if you and your very beautiful companions — are forced to remain here indefinitely. *(Salutes Girls, smiles and exits arch C. and L.)*

SHIRLEY. Well!

HARRY. *(Leans on piano.)* Did you hear that? He says he's a pawn.

BEBE. He's a Wop.

BEULAH. But he's cute!

SHIRLEY. Well, personally, I'd just as soon stay here. I'm sick of the slats on those stinking day coaches.

HARRY. Say, listen, after the way we've been betrayed in the

Balkans, we can't afford to stay any place. *(To Don.)* What's the matter, anyhow? *(Throws hat and briefcase on top of piano.)* Why can't decent people go about their own legitimate business?

DON.   Evidently you're not fully aware of the international situation?

HARRY.   I'm fully aware that the international situation is always regrettable ... *(Drops D. to chair L. of table D.L., sits.)* But what's wrong now?

DON.   Haven't you been reading the newspapers?

HARRY.   In Bulgaria and Jugo-Slavia? *(Turns to girls, who laugh.)* No!

EDNA.   Get *him!*

DON.   *(Amused, laughs, crosses L. to R. of table D.L.)* It may be difficult to understand, Mr. Van, but we happen to be on the brink of a frightful calamity.

HARRY.   What?

DON.   We're on the verge of war.

HARRY.   Yeah, I heard rumors — you mean like that business in Spain?

DON.   No, much more serious than that. All of them. World War.

HARRY.   But they just had one. *(Pittaluga appears on gallery, surveys crowd and starts coming down steps.)* Oh, no. I don't believe it. I don't believe —

PITTALUGA.   Do you wish rooms, Signor? *(Pittaluga comes downstairs to C. between Don and Harry. Don goes U. and crosses R., comes D.R. of Pittaluga.)*

HARRY.   Yeah, what've you got?

PITTALUGA.   We can give you grande de luxe accommodations, rooms with baths.

HARRY.   What's your scale of prices?

PITTALUGA.   From fifty lira up.

DON.   That's about five dollars a day.

HARRY.   What?

DON.   Meals included.

HARRY.   I take it there's the usual professional discount.

DON.   Oh, yes.

PITTALUGA. *(To Don.) Che cosa significa?*
DON. Mr. Van and the young ladies are artists.
PITTALUGA. *Ebbene?*
DON. In America we always give special rates to artists.
PITTALUGA. *Non posso, non posso. (The Cherrys appear on balcony above.)*
DON. *(Crosses L. below Pittaluga.)* I'm sure Signor Pittaluga will take care of you nicely, Mr. Van. He will show you attractive rooms on the other side of the hotel. They're delightful.
HARRY. No doubt. But I want to see the accommodations. *(Rises.)*
PITTALUGA. *(Goes U.C., stands L. end of arch.)* Step this way, please.
HARRY. *(Picks up hat and briefcase from piano.)* Now, listen, I want two girls to a room, and a single room for me adjoining. *(All rise except Beulah, who is busy putting on shoes.)* Come on, Beulah, put your shoes on. *(To Don.)* You see, Buddy, I promised their mothers I'd always be within earshot. *(Goes out U.C. and R. with Don, who goes L., preceded by Edna, Francine, Elaine and Bebe, Shirley with Beulah last. Pittaluga follows Harry out R.)*
BEULAH. *(As they go.)* I think this place is *attractive!*
SHIRLEY. *(As they exit through arch C.)* Aw, nuts!
HARRY. Nuts to you.
MRS. CHERRY. *(On top of stairs.)* Well, that's an extraordinary gathering!
CHERRY. *(L. of her.)* There's something I've never been able to understand — the tendency of Americans to travel en masse.
MRS. CHERRY. *(Looking about at room.)* This is a curious place, isn't it?
CHERRY. Yes, very!
MRS. CHERRY. It's a little bit dismal — don't you think so, Jimmy?
CHERRY. It's the Fascist idea of being desperately modern — Dynamic Symmetry! *(They pause to admire each other. He takes her in his arms.)* Darling!
MRS. CHERRY. What?
CHERRY. Nothing. I just said, "Darling!" My sweet. I love you.

21

MRS. CHERRY.   That's right. *(He kisses her.)*

CHERRY.   I think we're going to like it here, aren't we, darling?

MRS. CHERRY.   Yes.

CHERRY.   Even in spite of the dynamic symmetry?

MRS. CHERRY.   *(Turns R. toward view through window.)* You'll find a lot to paint.

CHERRY.   No doubt. But I'm not going to waste any time painting.

MRS. CHERRY.   Why not, Jimmy? You've got to work —

CHERRY.   Don't ask "why not" in that laboriously girlish tone! You know damned well why not!

MRS. CHERRY.   *(Laughing.)* Now really, darling. We're old enough to be sensible!

CHERRY.   God forbid that we should spoil everything by being sensible! This is a time for pure and beautiful foolishness. So don't irritate me by any further mention of work. *(Doctor enters from L. through arch C.)*

MRS. CHERRY.   Very well, darling. *(Cherry kisses her again. Doctor crosses R. to seat U.C. and regards their lovemaking with scant enthusiasm. They look down and see him. They aren't embarrassed.)*

CHERRY.   How do you do?

DOCTOR.   Don't let me interrupt you. *(Rings handbell on table below C. of seat U.C.)*

CHERRY.   It's quite all right. We were just starting out for a walk. *(Takes Mrs. Cherry by arm and they start coming downstairs. Dumptsy enters from R. through arch C., comes D. Quillery enters from R. through arch with a French magazine in his hand, comes D. to chair L. of table D.L., sits and reads. Quillery is a small, dark, brooding French extreme-left-radical Socialist.)*

DOCTOR.   *(To Dumptsy.)* Mineral water. *(Sits R. end of seat U.C.)*

DUMPTSY.   *Jawohl, Herr Doktor. (Starts L. for bar.)*

DOCTOR.   No ice — warm!

DUMPTSY.   *Herr Doktor. (Comes D. to table D.L., picks up Captain's glass, exits in bar.)*

MRS. CHERRY.   *(With Cherry R. of her. Speaks to Doctor.)* Isn't the air marvelous up here?

DOCTOR.   *Ja, ja. (A group of four Italian Flying Corps officers*

22

enters from L. through arch C., talking gaily in Italian.)

CHERRY.   Yes ... we think so. Come on, darling.   *(They wait until officers have passed through
arch, then exit through arch and L.)*
FIRST OFFICER.   *Sono Americane, eh?*
SECOND OFFICER.   *Forse sarrano stelle cine-
matografiche di Hollywood.*
FIRST OFFICER   *Ma sono tutte ragazze belle!*
THIRD OFFICER.   *Sono belle, ma proprio da far
strabiliare.*

*(All
spoken
together.)*

FOURTH OFFICER.   *E forse ora non ci rincrescera che hanno
cancellato tutta licenza. (They cross L. and exit into bar.)*
HARRY.   *(Enters from R. through arch C. He is chewing gum. To
Doctor.)* Good afternoon.
DOCTOR.   Good afternoon.
HARRY.   Have a drink?
DOCTOR.   I am about to have one.
HARRY.   Mind if I join you? *(Sits next and L. of Doctor on seat
U.C., takes out a small, silver snuff box, toys with it.)*
DOCTOR.   This is a public room. *(Dumptsy enters from bar L.,
crosses R., and serves Doctor with glass of mineral water.)*
HARRY.   It's a funny situation, isn't it?
DOCTOR.   *(Rises.)* To what situation do you refer?
HARRY.   All this stopping of trains ... and orders from Rome
and we on the threshold of a calamity.
DOCTOR.   To me it is not funny. *(Pays Dumptsy with coins. Takes
glass and starts for steps at R. Dumptsy crosses L. a few steps.)*
HARRY.   Scotch.
DUMPTSY.   With soda, sir?
HARRY.   Yes.
DUMPTSY.   Yes, sir.
QUILLERY.   *(Speaks with a French accent.)* I will have beer.
DUMPTSY.   We have native or imported, sir. *(Doctor goes up-
stairs.)*
QUILLERY.   Native will do.
DUMPTSY.   Yes, sir. *(Goes into bar L.)*

DOCTOR. *(On top of stairs.)* I repeat — to me it is *not* funny! *(He bows.)* You will excuse me.

HARRY. Certainly … See you later, pal. *(Doctor exits upper arch C. To Quillery.)* Friendly old bastard!

QUILLERY. Quite! But you were right. The situation is funny. There is always something essentially laughable about the thought of a lunatic asylum. Though, perhaps it is less humorous, when you are inside.

HARRY. I guess so. I guess it isn't easy for Germans to see the funny side of things these days. Do you mind if I join you? *(Rises and crosses to L.)*

QUILLERY. I beg of you to do so, my comrade.

HARRY. I don't want to thrust myself forward — but, you see, I travel with a group of blondes, and it's always a relief to find somebody to talk to. Have you seen the young ladies? *(Sits opposite Quillery on chair R. of table D.L.)*

QUILLERY. Oh, yes.

HARRY. Very alluring, aren't they?

QUILLERY. Very alluring. *(Dumptsy comes in with drinks, goes into bar again. Harry holds up snuff box, which he shows to Quillery.)*

HARRY. You know, that's a genuine antique snuff box, period of Louis Quinze.

QUILLERY. Very interesting.

HARRY. Yeah, a museum piece. *(Spits his chewing gum into snuff box, puts box into his pocket.)* You know, you've got to hoard your gum in Europe. — I've been a long way with that gorgeous array of beautiful girls. I took 'em from New York to Monte Carlo. To say we were a sensation in Monte Carlo would be to state a simple incontrovertible fact. But then I made the mistake of accepting an offer from the manager of the Club Arizona in Budapest. I found that conditions in the South East are not so good.

QUILLERY. I travelled with you on the train from Zagreb.

HARRY. Zagreb — oh, boy! What were you doing there?

QUILLERY. I was attending a Labor Congress.

HARRY. Yeah — I heard about that. The nightclub people thought that the congress would bring in business. They were wrong. But — excuse me — *(Rises.)* my name is Harry Van.

24

QUILLERY. *(Rises.)* Quillery is my name.

HARRY. Glad to know you, Mr. — ? *(They shake hands over table.)*

QUILLERY. Quillery.

HARRY. Quillery. *(Sits.)* I'm an American. What's your nationality?

QUILLERY. I have no nationality. *(Sits.)* I drink to your good health.

HARRY. Well — I drink to your lack of nationality, of which I approve. *(They drink. Signor and Signora Rossi enter from L. arch C. They have been skiing and are dressed in skiing clothes. He is a consumptive.)*

SIGNOR ROSSI. *Una bella giornata, Nina. Una bella giornata! Beviamo un po.*

SIGNORA ROSSI. *Dopo tutto quell' esercizio ti farebbe del male. Meglio riposarti per un'oretta.*

SIGNOR ROSSI. *Ma, se mi sento proprio bene. Andiamo. Mi riposero piu tardi. (They cross L. above Harry and Quillery, exit into bar where they are greeted ad lib. in Italian by officers.)*

HARRY. I always get an awful kick hearing Italian. It's beautiful. Do you speak it?

QUILLERY. Only a little. I was born a Frenchman.

HARRY. I see. You got over it.

QUILLERY. No. I loved my home. Perhaps if I had raised pigs — like my father, or his father before him, back to the time when Caesar's Roman legions came — perhaps, if I had done that, I would be a Frenchman, as they were. But I went to work in a factory — and machinery is international.

HARRY. I suppose pigs are exclusively French?

QUILLERY. Not all of them, but my father's pigs were! *(Harry laughs.)* The factory where I worked made artificial limbs. An industry that has been prosperous the last twenty years. But sometimes — in the evening — after my work — I would go out to the farm and help my father. And then, for a little while, I would become again a Frenchman.

HARRY. *(Takes out cigarette case.)* That's a nice thought, pal. *(Offers Quillery cigarette.)* Will you have a cigarette?

QUILLERY. No, thank you.

25

HARRY. I don't blame you. These Jugo-Slav cigarettes are not made of the same high-grade manure to which I became accustomed in Bulgaria.

QUILLERY. You know, my comrade — you seem to have a rather long view of things.

HARRY. So long it grows tiresome. *(Lights cigarette.)*

QUILLERY. The long view is not easy to sustain in this short-sighted world.

HARRY. You're right there, pal.

QUILLERY. Let me give you an instance. There we were — gathered at Zagreb, representatives of all the workers of Europe. All brothers, collaborating harmoniously for a United Front! And now — we are returning to our homes to prevent our people from plunging into mass murder — mass suicide!

HARRY. Oh, you're going back to France to stop the war?

QUILLERY. Yes.

HARRY. Do you think you'll succeed?

QUILLERY. Unquestionably! This is not 1914, remember! *(A ferocious-looking Major of the Italian Flying Corps enters from L. arch U.C. Crosses L. to bar.)* Since then, some new voices have been heard in the world — loud voices — I need only mention one of them — Lenin! Nicolai Lenin.

MAJOR. *(Bangs bar door open and shouts.) Attenti! (Officers in bar put their glasses down and stand at attention. Major exits into bar L.)*

HARRY. Yeah! — but what are you going to do about people like *that?*

QUILLERY. Expose them! That's all we have to do. Expose them — for what they are — atavistic children! Occupying their undeveloped minds playing with outmoded toys.

HARRY. Have you ever *seen* any of those toys?

QUILLERY. *Mais oui!* France is full of them. But there is a force more potent than all the bombing planes, the submarines, the tanks. It is the mature intelligence of the workers of the world! There is one antidote for war — Revolution! And the cause of Revolution gains steadily in strength. Even here in Italy, despite all this repressive power of Fascism, sanity has survived, and it becomes more and more articulate ...

HARRY. Well — you've got a fine point there, pal. And I hope you stick to it.

QUILLERY. I'm afraid you think it is all futile idealism!

HARRY. No — I don't. And what if I did? I am an idealist myself.

QUILLERY. You too believe in the revolution?

HARRY. Well, not exactly in *the* revolution. I'm just in favor of any revolution. Anything to wake people up, and give them some convictions. Have you ever taken cocaine?

QUILLERY. Why — I believe I have — at my dentists'.

HARRY. No — I mean, for pleasure. You know — a vice.

QUILLERY. No! I've never indulged in that folly.

HARRY. Well, I did once — during a stage of my career when luck was bad and confusion prevailed.

QUILLERY. Ah! You needed delusions of grandeur.

HARRY. That's just what they were.

QUILLERY. It must have been an interesting experience.

HARRY. It was illuminating. It taught me precisely what's the trouble with the world today. We've become a race of drug addicts — hopped up with false fears — false enthusiasms ... *(Three officers enter from bar L., talking excitedly, stand above Harry and Quillery.)*

SECOND OFFICER. *Ma, e state fatta la dichiarazone di geurra attuale?*

FIRST OFFICER. *Portere mo bombe esplosive?*

THIRD OFFICER. *Se la guerra ha veramente cominciatu, allora vuol dire che noi ...*

MAJOR. *(Enters from bar, followed by Fourth Officer.)* *Silencio! Solo il vostro commandante conosce gli ordini. Andiamo!*

FOURTH OFFICER. *Aspetta mi, Signor Maggiori, la guerra e cominciata il Italia e La Francia? (All above speeches are said together, as Major enters from bar L. All five hurriedly exit through arch C. and L. Aeroplane motors are heard off U.R.)*

QUILLERY. *(Jumps up.)* Mother of God! Did you hear what they were saying?

HARRY. *(Rises.)* I heard, but I couldn't understand.

QUILLERY. It was about war. I know only a little Italian — but I thought they were saying that war was already declared. I *must* go and demand that they let me cross the border! At once!

(Starts for arch C.)

HARRY.   Yeah, you've got no time to lose.

QUILLERY.   *(Comes D. to above table.)* Wait — I haven't paid — *(He is fumbling for money.)*

HARRY.   That's all right, pal. The drink's on me. *(Waves him off.)* Go on, go on!

QUILLERY.   Thank you, my comrade. *(Goes out quickly, U.C. through arch and L. Harry crosses R. to window and looks. Dumptsy enters from bar L. with tray, picks up empty beer glass and crosses R. to C.)*

DUMPTSY.   Fine view, isn't it, sir?

HARRY.   I've seen worse.

DUMPTSY.   Nothing quite like it, sir. From here, we look into four nations. Where you see that little village, at the far end of the valley — that is Austria. Isn't that beautiful over there?

HARRY.   *(Turns and looks at Dumptsy.)* Are you Italian?

DUMPTSY.   Well, yes, sir. That is to say, I didn't used to be. *(Aeroplane motors begin to dim out.)*

HARRY.   What did you used to be?

DUMPTSY.   Austrian. All this part was Austria, until after the big war, when they decided these mountains must go to Italy, and I went with them. *Ja,* in one day I became a foreigner. So now, my children learn only Italian in school, and when I and my wife talk our own language they can't understand us. *(Harry crosses L. to C. Dumptsy crosses L. to table D.L., gets Harry's drink and brings it over to him.)* They changed the name of this mountain. Monte Gabriele — that's what it is now. They named it after an Italian who dropped poems on Vienna. Even my old father, they got him, too. He's dead. But the writings on the gravestone was all in German, so they rubbed it out and translated it. So now he's Italian too. *(Harry takes Scotch from Dumptsy's tray.)* But they didn't get my sister. She married a Swiss. She lives over there, in Schleins.

HARRY.   *(Goes U. and sits C. of seat U.C.)* She's lucky.

DUMPTSY.   *(Goes U.L. of Harry.)* Ja ... those Swiss are smart.

HARRY.   Yeah, I wonder how the hell they ever got over there?

DUMPTSY.   *(Laughs dryly.)* But it doesn't make much difference who your masters are. When you get used to them, they're

28

all the same. *(Harry drains his glass. Porter's bell rings offstage, U.C. Pittaluga appears in arch C. from L.)*

PITTALUGA. Dumptsy! Dumptsy!

DUMPTSY. *Si, Padrone.*

PITTALUGA. *Una grande senora arriva. Prende i suoi bagaglio.*

DUMPTSY. *Si, signore. Vengo subito. (Puts tray, with beer glass on it, on table U. in nook, and exits arch C. and L.)*

PITTALUGA. *(Up in arch C., claps hands.) Affretati! Sciocco! Anna, Per Dio! (Anna, the maid, enters from R. and arch C.) Dove sei, stata va sopra preparare la stanza.*

ANNA. *Si, Si, venge.*

PITTALUGA. *Fa, presto, presto! (Anna hurriedly crosses R. below Harry, runs up steps, exits upper arch. Pittaluga comes D. to below arch C. and L. of it, stands there showing Irene in.)*

IRENE. *(Heard offstage, U.C.) Vieni, Achille.*

WEBER. *(Off.)* In a minute, my dear. *(He speaks English with a slight Continental accent.)*

DON. *(Enters from arch C., comes D.R. of arch.)* This is our cocktail lounge, Madame. *(Irene enters from arch C. She is somewhere between thirty and forty, beautiful, heavily and smartly furred in the Russian manner. Her hair is blond and quite straight. She is a model of worldly wisdom, chic, and carefully applied graciousness. She surveys the room with polite appreciation, glancing briefly at Harry. Irene is pronounced "Ear-ray-na." She speaks with a Russian accent.)* Your suite is up there, Madame. All this part of the hotel is new.

IRENE. *(Stands a moment in arch, then comes D.)* How very nice. *(Pittaluga exits into arch and L.)*

DON. We have our best view from this side of the hotel. *(Crosses R. below Harry to R. of steps. Irene crosses R. below Harry.)* From here we can look into four countries — Italy, Austria, Switzerland, and Bavaria.

IRENE. Magnificent!

DON. Yes — we're very proud of it.

IRENE. *(Goes up two steps to platform.)* All those countries. And they all look so very much alike, don't they?

DON. Yes — they do really — from this distance.

IRENE. All covered up with the beautiful snow. *(Goes U. to next landing.)* I think the whole world should be covered with snow.

It would be much more clean wouldn't it?

DON. By all means!

IRENE. Like in my Russia. White Russia. *(Dumptsy crosses from L. to R. at back with Weber's suitcase and two travelling cases of Irene's. Irene turns and looks through window.)* Oh, how exciting! A flying field. Look! They're bringing out the big bombers.

DON. You are interested in aviation, Madame?

IRENE. Just ordinary flying? Oh, no, it bores me. But there is no experience so thrilling as a parachute jump.

DON. *(Below her on stairs.)* I've never had that thrill, I'm ashamed to say.

IRENE. No? Once I had to jump when I was flying over the jungle.

DON. Really? Where?

IRENE. Indo-China. It was indescribable. Drifting down, sinking into that great green sea of enchantment and hidden danger.

DON. And you weren't afraid?

IRENE. Afraid? Oh, no, no. I was not afraid. In moments like that, one is given a sense of eternity. *(Harry viciously rings handbell on table in front of him. Dumptsy enters through arch C., picks up tray with beer glass.)*

IRENE. *(Her gaze wandering about the room.)* But your place is really quite charming.

DON. You're very kind, Madame.

IRENE. I must tell all my friends in Paris about it.

HARRY. Scotch!   *(Spoken together.)*

DUMPTSY. *(Strikes glass of Scotch from table at which Harry sits.)* Yes, sir. *(Starts to cross R.)*

HARRY. And I want some ice in it. If you haven't got any ice, scoop up some snow.

DUMPTSY. Yes, sir. *(Exits into bar L.)*

IRENE. *(Looking at L. wall.)* There's something about this design — it suggests a — an amusing kind of horror.

DON. *(Not knowing quite how to interpret that.)* You are a student of decoration, Madame? *(Goes up steps toward her.)*

IRENE.   Only an amateur, my friend. *(Air raid siren is heard off R.)* An amateur, I'm afraid, in everything. What is that?

DON.   It's just a sort of warning, Madame. They've been testing it.

IRENE.   A warning? Against what?

DON.   I think they installed it for use in case of war.

IRENE.   War? There will be no war. *(Pittaluga and Achille enter from L. and to arch C. Achille Weber is a thin, keen Frenchman wearing a neat little moustache and excellent clothes. Carries a leather portfolio under his arm. The name is pronounced "Vay-Bair.")*

PITTALUGA.   *Par ici, Monsieur Weber.*

Votre suite est par ici — (Crosses L. to first two steps, goes U., gestures to Weber to go U.)

(Spoken together.)

IRENE.   They are all too much prepared.

DON.   I'm sure of it, Madame.

IRENE.   Achille, Achille, there will be no war, will there?

WEBER.   No, no, Irene, there will be no war. *(Crosses R. to steps. Don comes down steps to platform.)* They're all much too well prepared for it.

IRENE.   *(To Don.)* There you are. See — they are all too much afraid of each other.

DON.   Of course, Madame. *(Achille goes up steps, followed by Pittaluga.)*

IRENE.   Achille, I'm mad about this place. *Je rafolle de cette place. (Starts upstairs.)*

WEBER.   Yes, my dear.

IRENE.   We must tell the Maharajah Rajpipla about this. How dear little "Pippi" will love it. *A droite — a gauche?*

PITTALUGA.   *A gauche,* Madame, *a gauche. (She exits upstairs into gallery, followed by Weber and Pittaluga. Harry rises, crosses L. as Don comes down steps and crosses L. to C.)*

HARRY.   *(His back to audience, looking U. after Irene.)* Who is that?

DON.   *(R. of Harry, his back to audience.)* That was Achille Weber. One of the biggest men in France. I used to see a great

31

deal of him at St. Moritz.

HARRY.   Who is the dame? Is that his wife?

DON.   *(Bristling.)* Are you implying that she's not?

HARRY.   No, no. I'm not implying anything. *(Goes U.C., then to piano.)* I'm just being kind of — baffled. *(Sits on piano bench. Sound of airplane motors from far off R. Dumptsy enters from bar and serves Harry with Scotch at piano.)*

DON.   Evidently! *(Goes U.C. and exits arch C. and L.)*

DUMPTSY.   *(Crosses R. to window.)* Do you see them — those aeroplanes — flying up from the field down there?

HARRY.   *(Glances toward window, without interest.)* Yes — I see them. *(Drinks Scotch in one gulp.)*

DUMPTSY.   Those are the big ones. They're full of bombs, to drop on people. Look! They're going north. Maybe Berlin. Maybe Paris. *(Harry strikes chord of any Russian folksong, perhaps "Kak Stranna."*)*

HARRY.   Did you ever jump with a parachute?

DUMPTSY.   Why, no — sir. *(He looks questioningly at Harry.)*

HARRY.   Well, I did — a couple of times. And it's nothing. But — I didn't land in any jungle. I landed in the Fair Grounds. *(Sound of aeroplanes begins to die out.)*

DUMPTSY.   *(Seriously.)* That's interesting, sir. *(Crosses L. to C. Signor and Signora Rossi enter from bar L. She is supporting him as they cross R. below Harry.)*

SIGNORA ROSSI.   *Non t'ho detto che devevi prender cura? Te l'ho detto.*

SIGNOR ROSSI.   *(In hoarse whisper.)* *Scusatemi,* Nina.

SIGNORA ROSSI.   *Te l'ho detto che accadrebbe cosi, or vedi, ti piglia un' accesso di tosse.* *(They go U.C. and exit through arch and L.)*

DUMPTSY.   *(Crosses L. to Harry at piano.)* That's Signor Rossi — he has tuberculosis.

HARRY.   He's getting cured up here? *(Doctor appears on gallery, smoking cigar, book under his arm. He starts coming downstairs.)*

DUMPTSY.   Pittaluga will ask him to leave when he finds out. This used to be a sanatorium in the old days. But the Fascisti, they don't like to admit that anyone can be sick! *(Crosses L.*

---

* See Special Note on Songs and Recordings on copyright page.

32

*below Harry toward bar as Harry starts playing any Russian folksong,
perhaps "Kak Stranna."*)*

DOCTOR.   *(On first landing.)* Dumptsy!

DUMPTSY.   *(Stops.) Wohl, Herr Doktor?*

DOCTOR.   Mineral water.

DUMPTSY.   *Gewiss, Herr Doktor? (Exits into bar. Doctor comes
downstairs, looks at Harry with some surprise.)*

DOCTOR.   What is that you're playing? *(Sits R. end of seat U.C.)*

HARRY.   A Russian song! One of those morose ballads about
how once we met, for one immortal moment, like ships that
pass in the night. Or, maybe like a couple of trucks side-swip-
ing each other. And now we meet again! How strange! A sentimental trifle. *(Dumptsy enters from bar, serves Doctor with mineral
water, Doctor pays him with coins, and Dumptsy crosses L. to table
D.L., picks up magazine L. by Quillery, stands at bar door listening
to music.)*

DOCTOR.   You're a musician?

HARRY.   Certainly. *(Stops playing the folksong and shifts into a
song like "When My Baby Smiles at Me."*)* I used to play the piano
in picture theatres — when that was the only kind of sound
they had — except the peanuts. *(Harry sings to accompaniment of
piano.)*

DOCTOR.   Do you know any Bach?

HARRY.   Bach? *(Stops playing.)* Certainly. *(Plays "Two Part In-
vention D Minor" by Bach, which he plays pretty badly.)*

DOCTOR.   You have good appreciation, but not much skill.

HARRY.   *(Stops the Bach.)* What do you mean, not much skill?
Listen to this. *(He goes into a trick arrangement of a song like "The
Waters of the Minnetonka."*)* Suitable for scenics — Niagara Falls
by moonlight. Or — *(He shifts into an Indian motif of same piece.)*
if you play it this way — it goes great with the scene where the
Indian chief turns out to be a Yale man. *(Shifts into a song like
"Boola Boola,"* then plays arpeggios.)*

DOCTOR.   Will you have a drink?

HARRY.   Oh! So you want me to stop playing?

DOCTOR.   No, no! I like your music very much.

* See Special Note on Songs and Recordings on copyright page.

HARRY.   Then in that case, I'd be delighted to have a drink with you ... Another Scotch, Dumptsy. *(Stops playing.)*
DUMPTSY.   Yes, sir. *(Exits into bar.)*
DOCTOR.   I'm afraid I was rude to you.
HARRY.   That's all right, pal. I've been rude to lots of people, and I never regretted it.
DOCTOR.   The fact is I am very gravely distressed.
HARRY.   I can see that, and I sympathize with you.
DOCTOR.   *(Fiercely.)* You cannot sympathize with me, because you do not know!
HARRY.   Perhaps not — except in a general way.
DOCTOR.   You are familiar with the writings of Thomas Mann. *(It is a challenge, rather than a question.)*
HARRY.   I'm afraid not, pal.
DOCTOR.   *(Opens book and reads.)* "Backsliding" — he said — "spiritual backsliding to that dark and tortured age — that, believe me, is disease! A degradation of mankind — a degradation painful and offensive to conceive." True words, eh?
HARRY.   Absolutely! *(Dumptsy enters from bar, places Scotch on R. end of piano and exits into bar.)*
DOCTOR.   Have you had any experience with the disease of cancer?
HARRY.   Certainly. I used to sell a remedy for it.
DOCTOR.   *(Exploding.)* There is no remedy for it, so far!
HARRY.   Well — this was a kind of remedy for everything.
DOCTOR.   I am within *that* of finding the cure for cancer! You probably have not heard of Fibiger, no?
HARRY.   I may have. I'm not sure. *(Lights cigarette.)*
DOCTOR.   He was a Dane — experimented with rats. He did good work, but he died before it was completed. I carry it on. I have been working with Oriental rats, in Bologna. But because of this war scare, I must go to neutral territory. You see, nothing must be allowed to interfere with my experiments. Nothing!
HARRY.   *(Rises, crosses R. to C., taking glass of Scotch with him.)* No. No. They're important.
DOCTOR.   The laboratory of the University of Zurich has been placed at my disposal — and in Switzerland, I can work, undisturbed. I have twenty-eight rats with me, all in various

34

carefully tabulated stages of the disease. It is the disease of civilization — and I can cure it. And now they say I must not cross the border.

HARRY. *(Laughs.)* You know, Doctor, it *is* funny.

DOCTOR. *What's* funny? To you, everything is funny!

HARRY. *(Sits L. of Doctor.)* No — I mean you and me being in the same fix. Both trying to get across that line — you with rats — me with girls. Of course, I realize that civilization at large won't suffer much if we get stuck in the war zone. Whereas with you, there's a lot at stake —

DOCTOR. It is for me to win one of the greatest victories of all time. And the victory belongs to Germany.

HARRY. Sure it does!

DOCTOR. *(Continues.)* Unfortunately, just now the situation in Germany is not good for research. They are infected with the same virus as here. Chauvinistic nationalism!

HARRY. Is that so?

DOCTOR. *Ja,* they expect all bacteriologists to work on germs to put in bombs to drop from aeroplanes, to fill people with death, when we've given our lives to *save* people. *Lieber Gott!* Why don't they let me do what is good? Good for the whole world? Forgive me, I become excited.

HARRY. No, I know exactly how you feel. You know, back in 1918, I was a shill for a carnival show, and I was doing fine. The boss thought very highly of me. He offered to give me a piece of the show, and I had a chance to get somewhere. And then what do you suppose happened? Along comes the United States Government and they drafted me! You're in the army now! They slapped me into a uniform and for three months before the Armistice, I was parading up and down guarding the Ashokan Reservoir. They were afraid your people might poison it. I've always figured that little interruption ruined my career. But I've remained an optimist, Doctor.

DOCTOR. *You* can afford to.

HARRY. No, I remained an optimist because I'm essentially a student of human nature. Now you dissect rats and corpses and similar unpleasant things. Well — it's been my job in life to dissect suckers! I've probed into the souls of some of the goddamndest specimens. And what have I found? Now, don't sneer at me, Doctor — but above everything else I've found Faith. Faith in peace on earth, good will to men — Faith that "Muma" — "Muma" the three-legged girl — really has got three legs. All my life I've been selling phoney goods to people of meagre intelligence and great faith. I suppose you'd think that would make me contemptuous of the human race? But — on the contrary — it has given *me* Faith. It's made me sure that no matter how much the meek may be bulldozed or gypped they will eventually inherit the earth. *(Shirley and Bebe enter from R. end of arch C.)*

SHIRLEY.   Harry!

HARRY.   What is it, honey?

SHIRLEY.   *(Crosses R. to Harry, hands him printed notice.)* Say, Harry, did you see this?

HARRY.   Allow me to introduce Miss Shirley Laughlin and Miss Bebe Gould.

SHIRLEY and BEBE.   How do you do?

DOCTOR.   *(Grunts.)* How do you do? *(Harry looks at notice.)*

SHIRLEY.   *(Sits L. of Harry.)* They got one of those things posted in each of our rooms.

HARRY.   *(Showing it to Doctor.)* Look — "What to do in case of air raids" — in all languages.

DOCTOR.   *Ja —* I saw that.

SHIRLEY.   Give it back to me. I'm going to send it home to Mama.

HARRY.   *(Handing it to her.)* Souvenir of Europe.

SHIRLEY.   It'll scare the hell out of her.

BEBE.   *(Standing L. of Shirley.)* Say, what's the matter with these people? Are they all screwy?

HARRY.   You hit it right on the nose, dear! *(Turns to Doctor.)* Oh, Doctor, these are very wonderful, very profound little girls. The mothers of tomorrow. *(Beulah enters R. end of arch C.)*

SHIRLEY.   Oh — shut up!

BEULAH.   Say — Harry …

HARRY.   Yeah, what do you want?

BEULAH.   Is it all right if I go out with Mr. Navadel and learn how to do this skiing? *(Weber comes out on gallery and starts down-*

stairs, takes cigar out of his case.)

HARRY. What? And risk breaking those pretty legs? Emphatically — no!

BEULAH. But it's healthy. *(Comes D.)*

HARRY. But not for me, dear. Those gams of yours are my bread and butter. *(Beulah goes U. and sits in corner U.C. Francine enters through from R. arch C. She and Bebe drop D. to seat D.L. and sit. Captain enters from L. through arch C., apparently alarmed about something. Francine and Bebe stare at him.)* Sit down, girls, and amuse yourself — with your own thoughts.

CAPTAIN. *(Crosses R. to Weber at below stairs, R.)* Monsieur Weber, I have been trying to get through to headquarters.

WEBER. And when can we leave?

CAPTAIN. Not before tomorrow, I regret to say. *(Irene appears on gallery.)*

WEBER. Signor Lanza in Venice assured me there would be no delay.

CAPTAIN. There would be none, if only I could get into communication with the proper authorities. But — the wires are crowded. The whole nation is in a state of uproar.

WEBER. Already? It's absurd lack of organization. *(Crosses L. below Captain to chair L. of table, D.L. Pianist and Drummer come in from U.C. and go on platform L. Violinist and Saxophonist follow. Irene comes downstairs.)*

CAPTAIN. *(Crosses L. after Weber.)* There is good excuse for the excitement now, Monsieur Weber. The report has just come to us that a state of war exists between Italy and France.

HARRY. What?

CAPTAIN. There is a rumor of war between Italy and France!

HARRY. Rumors — rumors — everything's rumors! When are we going to *know?*

CAPTAIN. *(Takes few steps U.C.)* You'll know soon enough.

DOCTOR. And what of Germany?

CAPTAIN. Germany has mobilized. *(Irene, at bottom of steps, pauses to listen.)* But I don't know if any decision has been reached. Nor do I know of the situation anywhere else. But — God help us — it will soon be serious enough for everyone on this earth.

IRENE. *(Crosses L. to table D.L. during Captain's speech. Weber rises.)* I thought you said there would be no war, Achille. Has there been some mistake somewhere? *(Sits chair above table D.L.)*

WEBER. There is only one way to account for it, my dear ... Spontaneous combustion of the dictatorial age. *(Sits chair L. of table D.L.)*

IRENE. How thrilling it must be in Paris at this moment! Just like 1914. All the lovely soldiers singing — marching — marching — *(Dumptsy enters from bar L., and stands above Weber, awaiting orders.)*

HARRY. What's the matter with the music? Us young folks want to dance. *(Elaine and Edna enter from R. through arch C. on last of Irene's speech.)*

IRENE. We must get across that border. We must get to Paris at once, Achille.

ELAINE. Harry, can I have a drink now?

HARRY. Yeah, sure, sit down anywhere. *(Spoken

WEBER. Will you have a drink, Irene? together.)*

IRENE. No. *(Musicians start playing.)*

BEBE. *(Calling to Edna.)* Edna?

WEBER. Will you, Captain Locicero?

CAPTAIN. Thank you. Brandy and soda, Dumptsy. *(Sits chair R. of table D.L.)*

DUMPTSY. *Si, Signor.*

WEBER. For me, Cinzano.

DUMPTSY. Cinzano? *Oui*, Monsieur. *(Exits into bar L. after Edna has crossed above him.)*

DOCTOR. It's all incredible.

HARRY. *(Rises.)* Yes, Doctor, but I still remain an optimist. *(Looks searchingly at Irene.)* Let doubt prevail throughout this night — with dawn will come again, the light of truth. *(Takes Shirley and begins to dance with her, always keeping his eyes on Irene. Don has entered from L. and arch C., and goes over to Beulah, begins to dance with her. Captain turns R. to watch dancing and catches sight of Shirley's posterior sticking way out and facing audience. Captain roars with laughter, as the curtain falls.)*

38

ACT TWO

Scene 1

Scene: The same.

About 7:30, evening of same day. Venetian blinds on the three windows are down.

The Cherrys are seated at seat upstage center, he right of her. Both are dressed for dinner. He is smoking a cigarette, as curtain rises. Auguste crosses right, serves them cocktails.

CHERRY.   Thank you. *(Puts coins on Auguste's tray.)* Has any more news come through?

AUGUSTE.   No, signor. They permit the radio to say nothing.

CHERRY.   I suppose nothing really will happen.

AUGUSTE.   Let us pray that is so, signor. *(Crosses L. and exits into bar.)*

CHERRY.   *(Leans over affectionately toward Mrs. Cherry.)* My sweet ... you're really very lovely.

MRS. CHERRY.   Yes. *(Cherry picks up glass and hands it to her, then picks up his glass.)*

CHERRY.   Here's to us, darling.

MRS. CHERRY.   And to hell with all the rest.

CHERRY.   And to hell with all the rest. *(They drink, solemnly.)*

MRS. CHERRY.   Jimmy —

CHERRY.   What is it, darling? *(Puts his drink down.)*

MRS. CHERRY.   Were you just saying that — or do you believe it?

CHERRY.   That you're lovely? I can give you the most solemn assurance ...

MRS. CHERRY.   No — that nothing is going to happen?

39

CHERRY. Oh.

MRS. CHERRY. Do you believe that?

CHERRY. I know this much: They can't start any real war without England. And no matter how stupid and blundering our government may be, our people won't stand for it.

MRS. CHERRY. But people can be such complete fools. *(Puts drink down.)*

CHERRY. I know it, darling. Why can't they be like us?

MRS. CHERRY. You mean — nice?

CHERRY. Yes — nice.

MRS. CHERRY. And intelligent.

CHERRY. And happy.

MRS. CHERRY. We are very conceited, aren't we?

CHERRY. Of course. And for good and sufficient reason.

MRS. CHERRY. Yes. I'm glad we're such superior people, darling. It's so comforting. *(Harry enters from R. through arch C., goes to piano.)*

CHERRY. Oh, hello. *(Harry, not wishing to intrude on them, starts for U.C. again.)* Oh, don't run away. Play something, won't you?

MRS. CHERRY. Won't you have a drink with us?

HARRY. *(Puts out his cigarette in ashtray on piano.)* No, thanks, Mrs. Cherry — if you don't mind. *(Sits at piano.)* I'm afraid I put down too many Scotches this afternoon. As a result of which I've had to treat myself to a bicarbonate of soda. *(Harry starts playing.)*

CHERRY. *(Sotto voce.)* I intend to get completely blotto. *(Drinks.)*

MRS. CHERRY. Oh, I love that!

HARRY. Thanks, Mrs. Cherry — always grateful for applause from the discriminating. *(Finishes the strain and stops.)*

MRS. CHERRY. Do play some more.

HARRY. No. The mood ain't right.

MRS. CHERRY. I can't tell you what a relief it is to have you here in this hotel.

HARRY. It's very nice of you, Mrs. Cherry. But I don't deserve your handsome tribute. Frequently I can be an asset at any gathering — contributing amusing anecdotes and bits of homely philosophy. But here and now, I'm not at my best.

CHERRY. You're the only one who seems to have retained any degree of sanity.

MRS. CHERRY. You and your young ladies.

HARRY. The girls are lucky. They don't know anything. *(Lights another cigarette with his lighter.)* And I guess the trouble with me is I don't give a damn.

MRS. CHERRY. We've been trying hard not to know anything — or not to give a damn. But it isn't easy.

HARRY. You haven't been married very long, have you? I hope you don't mind my asking ...

CHERRY. We were married the day before yesterday.

HARRY. Let me offer my congratulations.

CHERRY. Thank you very much.

HARRY. It's my purely intuitive hunch that you two ought to get along fine.

CHERRY. That's our intention, Mr. Van.

MRS. CHERRY. Yes. And we'll do it, what's more. You see — we have one supreme thing in common: We're both independent.

CHERRY. We're like you Americans in that respect.

HARRY. You flatter us.

MRS. CHERRY. Jimmy's been out in Australia, doing colossal murals for some government building. He won't show me the photographs of them, but I'm sure they're simply awful.

CHERRY. They're allegorical.

HARRY. At that I'll bet they're pretty good. *(Cherry laughs.)* What do you do, Mrs. Cherry?

MRS. CHERRY. I work in the gift department at Fortnum's —

HARRY. You mean behind a counter?

MRS. CHERRY. Yes — wearing a smock, and disgracing my family.

HARRY. Well, what d'ye know!

MRS. CHERRY. Both our families hoped we'd be married in some nice little church, and settle down in a nice little cottage, in a nice little state of decay. But when I heard Jimmy was on the way home I just dropped everything and rushed out here to meet him, and we were married in Florence.

CHERRY. We hadn't seen each other for nearly a year — so,

41

you can imagine, it was all rather exciting.

HARRY. Yeah, I can imagine.

MRS. CHERRY. Florence is the most perfect place in the world to be married in.

HARRY. I guess that's true of any place.

CHERRY. You see, we both happen to love Italy. And — well — we're both rather on the romantic side.

HARRY. You stay on that side, no matter what happens.

MRS. CHERRY. *(Quickly.)* I say, what do you think is going to happen?

HARRY. I haven't the slightest idea.

CHERRY. We've looked forward so much to being here with no one bothering us, and plenty of winter sports. You see, we're both keen on skiing. *(He pronounces it "she-ing." The English way.)* And now — we may have to go dashing back to England at any moment.

MRS. CHERRY. It's rotten luck, isn't it?

HARRY. Yes, Mrs. Cherry. It is rotten. *(Quillery enters from bar L., reading Italian newspaper.)* Any news?

QUILLERY. *(Glaring.)* News? Not in this patriotic journal! "Unconfirmed rumors" — from Vienna, London, Berlin, Moscow, Tokyo. And a lot of confirmed lies *(He slaps paper down on table D.L.)* from Fascist headquarters in Rome. *(Sits chair L. of table D.L.)*

CHERRY. I don't suppose one can get the truth anywhere — not even in the *Times*.

MRS. CHERRY. Perhaps it's just as well.

QUILLERY. If you want to know what is really happening, ask *him* — up there!

CHERRY. Who?

QUILLERY. Weber! The great Monsieur Achille Weber of the *Comité des Forges!* He can tell you all the war news. Because he *made* it. You don't know who he is? Or what he is doing here in Italy?

CHERRY. No.

QUILLERY. He is organizing the arms industry. Munitions. To kill French babies and English babies. *(Rises, goes U.C. to between Cherrys and Harry.)* France and Italy are at war. *(Doctor enters on balcony, comes D. to middle landing, listens.)* England joins France. Germany joins Italy. And that will drag in the Soviet Union and the Japanese Empire and the United States. In every part of the world the good desire of men for peace and decency is undermined by the dynamite of jingoism. And it needs only one spark, set off by one egomaniac, to blow it all up in one final explosion. *(He drops D. to chair L. of table D.L., sits during following speech.)* Then love becomes hatred, courage becomes terror, hope becomes despair. But — it will all be very nice for Achille Weber. Because he is a master of the one *real* League of Nations — The League of Schneider-Creusot, of Krupp, Skoda, Vickers and Dupont. The League of Death! *(Doctor slowly comes down rest of steps. Outburst.)* And the workers of the world are expected to pay him for it, with their sweat and their life's blood.

DOCTOR. *(R. of Cherry.)* Marxian nonsense!

QUILLERY. Ah! Who speaks?

DOCTOR. *I* speak.

QUILLERY. Yes! The eminent Dr. Hugo Waldersee. A wearer of the sacred swastika. Down with the Communists! Off with their heads! So the world may be safe for the Nazi murderers.

DOCTOR. So that Germany may be safe from its oppressors! It is the same with all of you — Englishmen, Frenchmen and the Marxists — you manage to forget that Germany, too, has a right to live! *(Rings handbell on table at R. end of seat U.C.)*

QUILLERY. If you love your Germany so much, why aren't you there now — with your rats?

DOCTOR. I am not concerned with politics. *(Auguste enters from bar, L.)* I am a scientist. *(To Auguste.)* Mineral water! *(Auguste bows, exits into bar. Doctor sits on seat U.C.R. of Cherry.)*

QUILLERY. A scientist — that's it, Herr Doctor! A servant of humanity! And you know, if you were in your dear Fatherland, the Nazis would make you abandon your cure for cancer. It might benefit too many people outside Germany — maybe even some Jews. *(Doctor lights cigar.)* They would force you to devote yourself to breeding malignant bacteria — millions of little germs, each one taught to give the Nazi salute ... *(Gives Nazi salute.)* and then go out and poison the enemy. *(Auguste enters from bar, serves Doctor with mineral water. Doctor puts some coins on his tray, and exits into bar.)* You — a fighter against disease and death — you could become a Judas goat in a slaughter house.

CHERRY.   I say, Quillery, old chap — do we have to have so much blood and sweat just before dinner?

QUILLERY.   *(Turning on him.)* Just before dinner! And now we hear the voice of England! *(Rises, crosses R. and U. to between Harry and piano, and the Cherrys.)* The great, well-fed, pious hypocrite! The grabber — the exploiter — the immaculate butcher! It was *you* who forced this war, because miserable little Italy dared to drag its black shirt across your trail of Empire. But what do you care if civilization goes to pieces — *(Don crosses from L. to R. at back, stops to listen in arch.)* so long as you have your dinner, and your dinner jacket!

CHERRY.   *(Rising.)* I'm sorry, Quillery, old chap — but I think we'd better conclude this discussion out on the terrace.

MRS. CHERRY.   Don't be a damned fool, Jimmy. You'll prove nothing by thrashing him.

QUILLERY.   It's the Anglo-Saxon method of proving everything! Very well — I am at your disposal. *(Cherry crosses L. below table at which he was sitting toward Quillery.)*

DON.   *(Quickly comes D. to between Cherry and Quillery.)* No! Please, Mr. Cherry. *(He turns to Quillery.)* I must ask you to leave if you can't conduct yourself as a gentleman.

QUILLERY.   Don't say any more. Evidently I cannot conduct myself properly. I apologize, Mr. Cherry.

CHERRY.   That's quite all right, old man. *(Offers hand and Quillery shakes it. Don goes U. to arch C.)* Have a drink.

QUILLERY.   No, thank you. My apologies, Herr Doctor.

DOCTOR.   There is no need for apologizing.

QUILLERY.   If I let my speech run away with me, it is because I have a hatred for certain things. And you should hate them, too. They are the things that make us blind — and ignorant, and dirty. *(Turns and goes out quickly U.C. arch and L. He is followed by Don.)*

MRS. CHERRY.   He's so right about everything.

CHERRY.   Yes, I know, poor chap. Will you have another cocktail, darling?

MRS. CHERRY.   No, I don't think so. Will you, Doctor? *(Doctor shakes head. Rises.)* Well, let's dine. *(Doctor drinks his water, then lets his eyeglasses hang on L. ear as he rubs his eyes.)*

CHERRY.   It will be a bit difficult to summon up much relish. *(They go out, hand-in-hand, U.C. and L.)*

HARRY.   *(Still seated at piano.)* I find these two very appealing, don't you, Doctor? Did you know they were only married the day before yesterday? Yeah, got themselves sealed in Florence — because they love Italy. They came up here hoping to spend their honeymoon on skis ... Kind of pathetic, isn't it?

DOCTOR.   *(After a short pause.)* What are you saying? *(Adjusts eyeglasses.)*

HARRY.   Nothing. I was only making conversation.

DOCTOR.   That Communist! *(Don appears in arch C.)* Making me a criminal because I am a German!

DON.   *(Comes D.L. of Doctor.)* I'm dreadfully sorry, Dr. Waldersee. We should never have allowed that insufferable little cad to come in here.

DOCTOR.   *(Rises.)* Oh — it's no matter. *(Crosses L. below Don.)* I have heard too many hymns of hate before this. To be a German is to be used to insults and injuries. *(Exits U.C. arch and L. Don starts to go out U.C.)*

HARRY.   Say, Don.

DON.   Yes?

HARRY.   Did you find out who that dame is?

DON.   What "dame"?

HARRY.   That Russian number — you know, the one with Weber.

DON.   I have not enquired as to her identity.

HARRY.   Did he register her as his wife?

DON.   They registered separately. And if it's not too much to ask, might I suggest that you mind your own damned business?

HARRY.   Yeah, you might suggest just that. And I would still be troubled by one of the most tantalizing of questions — "Where have I seen that face before?" Usually, it turns out to be somebody in the second row, one night yawning!

DON.   Yeah, I'm sure that such is the case right now. *(Starts U.C.)*

HARRY. Say, Don.

DON. *(Impatiently.)* Well, what is it?

HARRY. I take it your job around here is that of a professional greeter?

DON. You're at liberty to call it that, if you choose.

HARRY. I mean a sort of a YMCA secretary — I mean one that sees to it that everybody gets together and has a good time.

DON. Well?

HARRY. Well — do you think you're making a good job of it right now?

DON. Have you any suggestions for the improvement of the performance of my duties?

HARRY. Yes, Don — I have.

DON. *(Simply furious.)* I'd very much like to know just exactly who the hell you think you are to be offering criticism of my work ...

HARRY. Please, you needn't scream at me. I'm only trying to be helpful. I'm making you an offer.

DON. Well, what is it?

HARRY. *(Looks D.R.)* I see you've got a color wheel here.

DON. *(Turns R. and looks.)* Yes, yes. We use it during the supper dance. Now if you don't mind ...

HARRY. Well — yeah — how would it be if the girls and me put on part of our act tonight? For purposes of wholesome merriment — and to relieve the general tension?

DON. What kind of an act is it?

HARRY. Don't say "What kind of an act is it" in that tone. The act is good enough for this place. Those girls have played before the King of Roumania, and if my suspicions are correct — well, we won't pursue that subject. All that need concern you is that we can adapt ourselves to our audience, and tonight we'll omit the bubble dance and Bebe's shimmy with the detachable gardenias, unless there's a special request for it.

DON. Do you expect to be paid for this?

HARRY. Certainly not. I'm making this offer out of the goodness of my heart. Of course, if you want to make a little generous adjustment on our hotel bill ... *(Irene appears on gallery*

46

and starts to come D. She is wearing a dinner dress. Stops on lowest platform, peers through slats of Venetian blinds.)

DON. And you'll give me your guarantee that there'll be no vulgarity?

HARRY. *(Looks up, sees Irene. Don also turns and sees her.)* One more crack like that and the offer is withdrawn.

DON. *(Changes his tone entirely.)* Oh, I think it's a splendid idea, Mr. Van. I'm sure we'll all greatly appreciate your little performance. *(Crosses R. a few steps to Irene.)* Good evening, Madame. *(Harry rises, calms down.)*

IRENE. *(With the utmost graciousness.)* Good evening, Mr. Navadel. It is a lovely view. It is like a landscape on the moon. *(Crosses L. to C. seat U.C.)*

DON. Yes — yes. That's exactly what it's like.

HARRY. *(L. of Don, staring at Irene over Don's shoulder.)* Of course you realize we'll have to rehearse with the orchestra.

DON. Oh, yes — our staff will be completely at your disposal, Mr. Van. *(Harry goes U.C. to arch.)*

IRENE. What became of those planes that flew off this afternoon? I haven't heard them come back yet. *(Takes out long Russian cigarette from her purse.)*

DON. I expect they've gone to some base farther from the frontier. I certainly hope so. They used to make the most appalling racket. *(Lights cigarette for her.)*

HARRY. About eleven o'clock? *(Exits through arch C. and R. Weber appears on gallery, smoking a cigar. He is not in evening dress. Comes downstairs and also peers through blinds.)*

DON. Yes, Mr. Van. Eleven o'clock will do nicely. Could I bring you a cocktail, Madame?

IRENE. Vodka, if you please.

DON. Vodka? Why, certainly, I shall have it sent right in. *(Crosses L., exits into bar.)*

WEBER. A perfectly cloudless night. They are very lucky.

IRENE. *(Sits C. of seat U.C.)* Did you get your call?

WEBER. *(Comes D., crosses L.)* Yes. I talked with Lanza.

IRENE. The news was I suppose as usual — very good.

WEBER. *(Sits R. of Irene.)* It is extremely serious! You saw those bombers that left here this afternoon?

47

IRENE. Yes.

WEBER. They were headed for Paris. Italy is evidently in a great hurry to deliver the first blow.

IRENE. How soon may we leave here?

WEBER. None too soon, I can assure you. The French High Command will know that the bombers came from this field. There will be reprisals.

IRENE. Huh!

WEBER. — probably within the next twenty-four hours.

IRENE. That will be exciting to see.

WEBER. An air raid?

IRENE. What — here? — with the bombs bursting in the snow? Sending up great geysers of diamonds?

WEBER. Or perhaps great geysers of us.

IRENE. I suppose many people in Paris are now being killed.

WEBER. I am afraid so. Unless the Italians bungle it.

IRENE. Perhaps your sister — Madame d'Hilaire — and her darling little children — *ils sont tous morts. C'est vraiment terrible!*

WEBER. No, no, Irene. Don't talk French. Your French is worse than your Russian.

IRENE. Not so bad as my Cockney. *(Drops Russian accent and goes into Cockney dialect.)* You should have heard my Cockney: *(Begins to sing in Cockney dialect.)* "If those lips could only speak —"

WEBER. *(Admonishing her.)* Irene!

IRENE. "And those eyes could only see — And those beautiful golden tresses —"

WEBER. Someone will hear you. Stop, stop it, Irene.

IRENE. I have stopped.

WEBER. I prefer you Russian — as you were when I first met you. Two years ago now, isn't it, Irene?

IRENE. Four years ago, Achille. Thank you very much.

WEBER. Yes! I greatly prefer you Russian.

IRENE. *(In plain English — without any dialect.)* I know. Russian makes me more mysterious. A Russian accent gives me a romantic past. They think: "Perhaps I'm a daughter of the Czar — or a spy or something." At any rate they have to watch me. Oh, Achille, I don't want you to be ashamed of me. And I know when I talk English, however well, sooner or later some Cockneyism pops out. And then everybody knows me for what I am — a London guttersnipe — with a piquant dash of Armenian. Just — nobody.

WEBER. My dear, you could never be nobody.

IRENE. Everybody can be nobody by merely removing their masks. But I know you prefer people with their masks on. So I shall continue with my Russian. *(Resumes Russian accent.)* It is the easiest for me. I have been doing it for so long, now. *(Dumptsy enters with glass of vodka, book of waiter's checks and small pencil on tray, from bar L. Crosses R., serves vodka.)*

WEBER. *(Rises, crosses L. below Irene as Dumptsy crosses R.)* I shall telegraph to Joseph to have the house ready. *(He signs check on Dumptsy's tray.)* It will be rather cold in Biarritz now — but far healthier than in Paris. Am I right?

IRENE. Oh, Achille.

WEBER. You are going to dinner now?

IRENE. Yes.

WEBER. I shall join you later. *(He goes out U.C. and L. Dumptsy picks up the Cherrys' glasses.)*

DUMPTSY. We will have a great treat tonight, Madame.

IRENE. Really?

DUMPTSY. That American impresario, that Mr. Harry Van — he will give us an entertainment with his dancing girls.

IRENE. Is he employed here regularly? *(Drinks vodka in one neat gulp.)*

DUMPTSY. Oh, no, Madame. He is just passing, like you. This is a special treat. It will be very fine.

IRENE. Let us hope so.

DUMPTSY. Madame is Russian, if I may say so.

IRENE. *(Pleased.)* What makes you think that I am Russian, h-m? Is it because I am drinking vodka?

DUMPTSY. Oh, no, Madame. Many people try to drink vodka. But only true Russians can do it gracefully. You see — I was a prisoner with your people in the war.

IRENE. So?

DUMPTSY. I liked them.

IRENE. You're very charming. What is your name?

DUMPTSY. I am called Dumptsy, Madame.

IRENE.   Dumptsy! You are going again to the war, Dumptsy?
DUMPTSY.   If they tell me to, Madame.
IRENE.   You will like being a soldier?
DUMPTSY.   Yes — if I'm taken prisoner soon enough.
IRENE.   I see. Tell me — who do you think will win?
DUMPTSY.   I cannot think, Madame. It is all very doubtful.
But one thing I can tell you, Madame. Whoever wins, it will be
the same as last time — Austria will lose. *(The Cherrys come in
from L.C. arch — come D. to table D.L.)*
IRENE.   Austria will lose, and they will all lose. *(She greets Cherrys pleasantly.)* Good evening.
CHERRY.   Good evening, Madame. *(Draws chair L. of table D.L.
Mrs. Cherry sits on it.)*
IRENE.   *(To Dumptsy.)* Bring me some more vodka. Perhaps Mr.
and Mrs. Cherry will have some, too.
CHERRY.   ... To tell you the truth, Madame —
MRS. CHERRY.   I'd love to. I've never tasted vodka.
IRENE.   Ah — then it is high time. Bring in the bottle.
DUMPTSY.   Yes, Madame. *(Exits into bar.)*
IRENE.   Come and sit down over here. *(Mrs. Cherry rises, they
cross R. to seat U.C. Mrs. Cherry sits R. of Irene, Cherry stands L. of
Irene.)* You know, vodka is the perfect stimulant to the appetite.
It is so much better than that hybrid atrocity, the American
cocktail!
CHERRY.   To tell you the truth, Madame — we've already
dined.
IRENE.   Then it is just as good as a liqueur.
MRS. CHERRY.   We didn't really dine at all. We merely looked
at the minestrone and the parmesan cheese — we felt too de-
pressed to eat anything.
IRENE.   I know. It is the altitude. *(Dumptsy enters from bar with
bottle of vodka and three more glasses already poured, places them on
table, crosses L., picks up newspaper which Quillery left on table D.L.,
exits into bar.)* After the first exhilaration there comes a depres-
sive reaction, especially for you, who are accustomed to the
heavy Pickwickian atmosphere of England.
CHERRY.   *(Sits L. of Irene.)* Oh — you know England, Madame?
IRENE.   *(Fondly.)* Of course I know England! My governess was

50

a sweet old ogre from your north country — and when I was a very little girl I used to visit often at Sandringham.

CHERRY. *(Impressed.)* Sandringham?   *(Spoken*
MRS. CHERRY. The palace?   *together.)*

IRENE. Yes. That was before your time, my dear. In the days of King Edward, and the beautiful Alexandra. *(Sighs a little for those days.)* I used to have such fun playing with my cousin David. Of course, I was much smaller than he. And when he tried to teach me to play cricket, and I could not swing the bat properly, he would say, "Oh, you Russians, you will never be civilized!" *(Cherry laughs.)* When I went home to Petersburg I told my uncle, the Tsar, what David had said, and he was so amused! But come now — you must drink your vodka. *(They rise, lift their glasses.)* A toast! To his most gracious majesty the King! *(They clink glasses.)* God bless him! *(All three drink, Mrs. Cherry coughs. Irene to Mrs. Cherry.)* No — no! Drink it right down. *Comme ça!* *(She swallows it in a gulp as do the Cherrys.)* Poor little child! The second glass will go more easily. *(Refills glasses from bottle as they sit.)* I used to laugh so at your funny British Tommies in Archangel. How they all hated vodka, until one of them thought of mixing it with beer.
MRS. CHERRY. How loathsome!
IRENE. It was! But I shall be forever grateful to them — those Tommies. They saved my life when I escaped from the Soviets. For days and nights — I don't know how many — I was driving through the snow — snow — snow — snow — it was, in a little sleigh, with the body of my father beside me, and the wolves running along like an escort of dragoons. You know — you always think of wolves as howling constantly, don't you?
CHERRY. Why, yes — I suppose one does.
IRENE. Well, they don't. No, these wolves don't howl! They are horribly, confidently silent. I think silence is so much more terrifying, don't you?
CHERRY. Yes! You must have been terribly afraid.
IRENE. No, I was not afraid — not for myself. No, it was the thought of my father ...

MRS. CHERRY. Please! I know you don't want to talk about it any more.

IRENE. Oh, no — it is so long ago now. But I shall never forget the moment when I came through that haze of delirium, and saw the faces of your Tommies! Those simple, friendly faces. And the snow — and the wolves — and the terrible cold — p-s-s-t! they was all gone and I was looking at Kew Gardens on a Sunday afternoon, *(Weber comes in from L. and U.C., comes D.)* with the sea of golden daffodils — "fluttering and dancing in the breezes."

WEBER. Shall we go in to dinner now, Irene? *(Cherry rises.)*

IRENE. What is that poem — Yes, yes, all right, Achille. *(Weber exits arch U.C. and L. Irene and Mrs. Cherry rise, pick up glasses.)* Now, remember — *(They lift their glasses.)* Go! *(All three drink. To Mrs. Cherry.)* You feel better now?

MRS. CHERRY. Yes, Madame.

IRENE. And now you must make another try to eat something.

CHERRY. *(Picks up Irene's purse on table.)* Thank you so much, Madame.

IRENE. And later on, we must all be here for that Mr. — ? What's his name?

CHERRY. Van?

IRENE. Van's entertainment — and we must all applaud vigorously. *(Crosses a few steps L. toward Cherry, who gives her back her purse.)*

MRS. CHERRY. We shall, Madame.

CHERRY. He's such a nice chap, isn't he?

IRENE. *(Crosses L. to Cherry.)* Oh, yes — and a real artist, too. *(Mrs. Cherry crosses to L. of Irene.)*

CHERRY. Oh — you're seen him? *(The three turn U.C. and start for arch C.)*

IRENE. Oh, yes — I've seen him somewhere. In some *café chantant,* somewhere. I forget just where it was. You know when you are travelling *(Curtain starts down.)* ... you don't know if it is Wednesday or Rome or what —

CURTAIN

Scene 2

Scene: The same. About eleven o'clock. Table downstage left has been placed downstage right, below right end of seat upstage center. There are two side chairs, left and right of table.

At rise: Weber is sitting in chair left of table downstage right, sipping brandy. Captain is standing right, above table downstage right, hat in hand.

CAPTAIN. Monsieur Weber, the situation is puzzling and alarming!

WEBER. You have received no *definite* news?

CAPTAIN. I have been listening to the radio. Utter bedlam! Of course, every government has imposed the strictest censorship — but they can't silence the intimation of chaos. It is very frightening — like one of those films where ghostly hands suddenly reach in and switch off all the lights.

WEBER. Any suggestion of air raids?

CAPTAIN. None — but there is ominous quiet from Paris. Think of it — Paris — utterly silent! Only one station there is sending messages, and they are in code.

WEBER. Probably instructions to the frontier.

CAPTAIN. I heard a man in Prague saying something that sounded interesting, but him I could not understand. Then I turned to London, hopefully, and listened to a gentleman describing the disastrous effects of ivy upon that traditional institution, the oak tree.

WEBER. Well — we shall soon know ... There'll be no trouble about crossing the frontier tomorrow?

CAPTAIN. Oh, no, Monsieur Weber. Except that I am still a little worried about Madame's passport. *(A faint sound of airplanes heard approaching.)*

WEBER. We'll arrange about that. *(Takes out leather cigar case.)* Have a cigar, Captain?

CAPTAIN. No, thank you.

IRENE. *(Appears at top of stairs, smoking a long, Russian cigarette, comes down.)* Do you hear the sound of airplanes, Captain? *(All stop to listen, intently. Captain dashes to window D.R., looks upward through Venetian blind.)*

CAPTAIN. It is our bombers. One — two — three. Seven of them. Seven out of eighteen. You will excuse me? *(Salutes, dashes out U.C. arch and L.)*

WEBER. Seven out of eighteen! Not bad, for Italians.

IRENE. *(Standing on platform, two steps up. Speaks clear English.)* I'm so happy for you, Achille.

WEBER. What was that, my dear?

IRENE. I said — I'm so happy for you.

WEBER. Happy? Why? *(He smiles.)*

IRENE. All this great, wonderful death and destruction. And you promoted it!

WEBER. Don't give me too much credit, Irene. *(Sounds of airplanes begins to die out.)*

IRENE. But I *know* what you've done.

WEBER. Yes, my dear. You know a great deal. But don't forget to do honor to Him — up there — who put fear into man. I am but the humble instrument of His divine will.

IRENE. *(Looking upward, sympathetically.)* Yes — that's quite true. We don't do half enough justice to Him. Poor, lonely old soul. Sitting up in heaven, with nothing to do but play solitaire. Poor, dear God. Playing Idiot's Delight. The game that never means anything, and never ends.

WEBER. What an engaging fancy you have, my dear.

IRENE. Yes.

WEBER. It is the quality in you that fascinates me most. Limitless imagination! It is what has made you such an admirable, brilliant liar. Am I right? *(Cuts end of cigar with cutter.)*

IRENE. Of course you are right. Had I been bound by any stuffy respect for the truth, I should never have escaped from the Soviets.

WEBER. I'm sure of it.

IRENE. Did I ever tell you of my escape from the Soviets?

WEBER. You have told me about it at least eleven times. And each time it was different. *(Lights cigar.)*

IRENE. Oh, well, that is because I have made several escapes.

(Comes D.R. of table D.R., sits opposite Weber.) I am always making escapes, Achille. When I am worrying about you, and your career. I have to run away from the terror of my own thoughts. So I amuse myself by studying the faces of the people I see. Just the ordinary, little people. *(She is speaking in a tone that is sweetly sadistic.)* That young English couple, for instance. I was watching them during dinner, sitting close together, holding hands, and rubbing their knees together under the table. And I saw him in his nice, smart, British uniform, shooting a little pistol at a tank. And the tank rolled over him. And his fine strong body, that was so full of the capacity for ecstasy, was a mass of mashed flesh and bones — a smear of purple blood — like a stepped-on snail. But before the moment of death, he consoled himself by thinking, "Thank God *she* is safe. She is bearing the child I gave her, and he will live to see a better world." But I know where she is. She is lying in a cellar that has been wrecked by an air raid, and the embryo from her womb is splattered against the face of a — dead bishop? That is the kind of thought with which I amuse myself, Achille. And it makes me very proud to think I am so close to you — who make all this possible.

WEBER.   Do you talk in this whimsical vein to many people?

IRENE.   No. I betray my thoughts to nobody but you. You know I am shut off from the world. I am a contented prisoner in your ivory tower.

WEBER.   *(Rises, crosses L. a few steps.)* I'm beginning to wonder about that.

IRENE.   Why? You think I could interest myself in somebody else?

WEBER.   *(Crosses R. to table D.R.)* No — my dear. I am merely wondering whether the time has come for you to turn commonplace, like all the others?

IRENE.   The others?

WEBER.   All those who have shared my life. My former wife now boasts that she abandoned me because part of my income is derived from the sale of poison gas. Revolvers and rifles and bullets she did not mind — because they are used also by sportsmen. Battleships, too, are permissible; they look so splendid in the news films. But she could not stomach poison gas.

(Goes U., drops ashes in ashtray on table R. end of seat U.C.) So now she is married to an anemic Duke, and the large fortune that she obtained from me enables the Duke to indulge his principal passion, which is the slaughtering of wild animals, like rabbits, and pigeons and rather small deer. My wife is presumably happy with him. I am glad you are not a fool as she was, Irene.

IRENE. No. I don't care for battleships. And I shall not marry an anemic Duke.

WEBER. *(Goes above table D.R.)* But — there is something a little reminiscent in the gaudy picture you paint of a wrecked cellar. I gather that this young couple has touched a tender spot, eh?

IRENE. Oh, Achille!

WEBER. Apply your intelligence!

IRENE. I do!

WEBER. *(Quietly, but with rapier-like thrusts.)* Ask yourself: Why shouldn't they die? And who are the greater criminals — those who sell the instruments of death, or those who buy them, and use them? You know there is no logical reply to that.

IRENE. No.

WEBER. But all these little people like your new friends — they all consider me an arch-villain because I furnish them with what they want — the illusion of power. Big guns — to protect them from the consequences of their own obvious inferiority! That is what they vote for in their pious governments, *(Crosses L. a few steps.)* what they cheer for on their national holidays — what they glorify *(Crosses R. a few steps.)* in their anthems, and their monuments, and their waving flags! They shout bravely about something they call "national honor"! And what does it amount to? Mistrust of the motives of everyone else! Dog in the manger defense of what they've got, and greed for the other fellow's possessions! Honor! — Honor among thieves! I assure you, Irene — that for such *little* people the deadliest weapons are the most merciful. *(Cherry is heard singing off L. and arch C. "I went down to St. James infirmary.")* I hoped I would never have to explain such obvious things to you. And now I must go up — and see about — *(Mr. and Mrs. Cherry enter from L. and arch C. He L. of her. They are in high spirits now. Auguste enters from bar.)*

56

IRENE. *(Puts out cigarette. Resumes Russian accent.)* Ah! Mr. and Mrs. Cherry!

CHERRY. Hello, there! *(They come D.L. of table D.R. Auguste crosses R. to L. of table below C. of seat U.C.)*

IRENE. You have dined well?

MRS. CHERRY. Superbly!

CHERRY. We ate everything — up to and including the zabaglione.

IRENE. You may thank the vodka for that. Vodka never fails in an emergency. *(Lights another cigarette.)*

CHERRY. We do so, and we thank you, Madame.

IRENE. May I introduce Monsieur Weber. Mr. and Mrs. Cherry. *(Ad lib. "How do you do's" from the Cherrys and Weber. Don, in dinner jacket, enters from L. and arch C., comes D.L. of group.)*

DON. *Bon soir,* Madame, Monsieur Weber. We're going to have a little cabaret show for you now, Madame. *(Goes U.C. arch, looks off R. Musicians enter from L. through arch C. and go on platform, take their places.)*

WEBER. I don't think I shall wait for it, my dear.

IRENE. But you must. — Please, Achille. Mr. Van is a real artist. You will be so amused.

WEBER. *(Sits opposite her at table D.R.)* Very well, Irene. *(Cherry orders two demi-tasses from Auguste. Auguste comes D. to above Weber, who gives his order for one brandy. Auguste bows, crosses L. above Don, exits into bar.)*

DON. *(Comes D. to table D.R., his tone blandly confidential.)* I can't vouch for the quality of the entertainment. But it may be unintentionally amusing.

IRENE. We shall love it.

CHERRY. *(Going U.C. with Mrs. Cherry to seat U.C.)* I think it's a splendid idea, Mr. Navadel.

DON. Oh, thank you. We try to contrive some novelty for our guests each evening. Won't you sit down? *(Cherry sits L. of Mrs. Cherry. Don goes U. to arch C. as the Rossis enter from L. and arch C., in evening clothes. Signor Rossi is L. of Signora Rossi and she is holding him by the arm. Auguste enters from bar with two demi-tasses and a liqueur glass on tray, crosses R.)*

CHERRY. *(Takes out cigarette case, offers it to Mrs. Cherry.)* Have

57

a cigar, darling? *(Laughs, takes a cigarette for himself. Following conversations go on simultaneously as Cherry speaks to Irene, Don speaks to Rossis, Dumptsy speaks with Doctor. To Irene.)* Do you have any zabaglione in Russia?

IRENE. No, that is purely an Italian dish. Do you like it?

CHERRY. Yes, very much.

MRS. CHERRY. I don't. *(Auguste serves Cherrys with coffee and, after Doctor and Dumptsy cross he comes D., serves Weber with liqueur, crosses L. and stands L. of Doctor.)*

DON. *(As he shows Rossis to seat D.L. below bar.)* Signor Rossi — Signora — prego — vienti qui —

ROSSI. *Ah, Signor Navadel! Buona serra. Grazie, grazie per l'invitazione.*

DON. *Buona appetita — sta serra?*

ROSSI. *Si, si, mangia bene sta serra.*

DON. *Buona.*

SIGNORA ROSSI. *Verrano teatro di Stati Uniti?*

DON. *Si, come piccolo teatro Americano.*

ROSSI. *(To Don.) Successo, signor, successo! (To Signora Rossi.) Sedetevi, chrina. (They sit. Doctor appears arch C. from L. and Dumptsy with two chairs nested together bumps into him.)*

DUMPTSY. *Entschuldigen Sie, Herr Doktor.*

DOCTOR. *Schon wider was los?*

DUMPTSY. *Heut' was ganz Spezielles der Mr. Van und seine Tanzmadels, Gott! hat der flinke Beine. Pst! Pst! Es wird Ihnen glanzend gefallen Herr Doktor.*

DOCTOR. *Jawohl! (He sits R. of Cherrys on seat U.C. Dumptsy places chairs round table D.R. below steps and Pittaluga comes down to superintend. Harry enters from R. through C. arch, wearing a dinner jacket. Don stands at R. of piano.)*

HARRY. *(In arch.)* All set, Don?

DON. Quite ready whenever you are.

HARRY. Are the lights OK?

DON. Yes, everything is ready.

HARRY. Give me a spot and a little fanfare. You know a little — tra — tra — tra.

DON. *(Turns to leader.)* A fanfare, please. *(Musicians play a fanfare. The spot goes on and lights go off. Anna, the maid, comes out on balcony and watches the show.)*

HARRY. *(Makes entrance, on which there is considerable applause. Puts straw hat and swagger stick on top of piano.)* Before we begin, folks, I just want to explain that we haven't had much chance to rehearse with my good friend, Signor Palota, and his talented little band here. *(Applauds. Palota rises and bows. All onstage applaud. He indicates orchestra, and applauds. Everyone onstage applauds, too.)* So — we must crave your indulgence and beg you to give us a break if the rhythm isn't all strictly kosher.

DON. *(Laughs heartily.)* Ho — ho — ho.

HARRY. Thank you very much. *(Shakes Don's hand.)* All we ask of you, kind friends, is "The Christian pearl of Charity," to quote our great American poet, John Greenleaf Whittier. *(Applauds. Everyone onstage applauds.)* Oakie-dokie, Signor, takes it away.

ROSSI. *(To Harry.)* Successo, signor! *(Pittaluga crosses L. to arch C., exits arch and R. Music starts playing, and Harry begins singing. [Production Note: At this point Harry sings part of a song. This is the beginning of a song-and-dance routine. The choice is left to the producer, who may use some original song, or perhaps the original or adaptation of music which is out of copyright.] After first verse sung by Harry, lights go on as Girls in costume appear three by three in arch C. Girls go into a dancing routine as Harry crosses L. below them and U. to below piano, keeps time to music by hitting top of piano. During the number Pittaluga, from L, enters, followed by Captain, First Officer, Major and Third Officer.)*

PITTALUGA. *Stiamo dando un trattenimento di gala, Capitano!*

CAPTAIN. *Ah, che — belle ragazze!*

PITTALUGA. *Potrebbe divertir voi E I vostri compagni, De guardare — Questo apettacolo.*

CAPTAIN. *Ma proprio — !*

HARRY. *(Crosses R. through line of girls to C., holds up hand and stops music.)* Customers, customers — *(To Captain, who has come D.C., with Officers following.)* What's up, Captain?

CAPTAIN. Some of my friends have come here to admire your art.

HARRY. *(To Captain.)* Tell the boys to sit down. *(To Violinist.)* Give the boys a little "Tra — tra." *(Captain and Officers cross R.*

59

*to table, followed by Pittaluga. Dumptsy crosses L. below groups, exits
into bar. Orchestra strikes up the Fascist song "Giovenneza"* and the
Captain and Officers at table D.R. raise their arms in Fascist salute.
The Rossis also rise and give salute. Cherry and Don rise and stand
at attention. Girls try to imitate the Officers' salute by waving their
arms. After song the music segues into the dance, Girls resume their
dancing and Officers sit at table D.R. Captain stands on platform of
stairs, two steps up. Pittaluga, after showing Officers to their places,
exits arch C. and L. and returns immediately with two more chairs
nested together, which he brings D. to their table, then crosses L. to arch
and greets Second and Fourth Officers, who drift in. The dance over,
Dumptsy enters from bar with demi-tasse and sugar and creamer on
tray — crosses R. below Girls and serves Doctor. There is applause from
everyone onstage and music segues into "Swanee River." [Traditional
melody here.] Harry crosses R. through Girls and begins to sing:)*

> They used to sing the Swanee River
>> And old Black Joe.
> They used to do the soft shoe essence
>> But that was long, long ago.
> They left their Mammies — Mammy!
>> Down in Dixie
>> And they began to roam.
> Now they're a lot of Harlem nuttin's
>> Far from the old folks at home.

*(Harry and Girls go into a soft shoe dance to the tune of "Swanee
River.")*

> Now they're a lot of Harlem nuttin's
>> Far from the old folks at home.

*(As drummer accentuates last note, Harry does a bump. They go into
a dance routine at the end of which Girls pick Harry up and take him
off into bar L. Harry throws kisses to his audience as Girls are taking
him off. As he passes Rossi he shakes hands with him. Much applause*

---

* This is out of print now, and hard to find. There should be no difficulty in substituting almost any melody not familiar to the average
audience.

onstage and particularly from Officers, who rise and shout "Bravo" —
"Bravissima" — "Bis," and stamp their feet with enthusiasm. Girls
reenter from bar, followed by Harry. They bow and exit U. arch C. as
Harry gyrates like a cheerleader, bringing on more applause. As Girls
go U.C. Dumptsy, followed by Auguste, crosses L. below groups, exits
into bar. During applause Officers at D.R. ad lib., and indicate to
Captain would he ask Harry to let the Girls sit down with them?)
CAPTAIN. *(Crosses L. to Harry at C.)* My friends wish to know
respectfully if the young ladies would care to join them in a little drink?
HARRY. Why, certainly! *(During this Palota, the pianist, rises,*
puts his sheet music on top of piano, gets off platform and stands
above it. Lights focussed on piano now slowly dim up.)
CAPTAIN. *(Crosses R. to Officers.) Sarrano con noi subito.*
HARRY. Come on in, girls. *(Girls enter from R. and arch C., led*
by Elaine.)
ELAINE. Say, Harry, what do we do now?
HARRY. *(Indicates Officers D.R.)* Join the army! *(Elaine, Francine*
and Bebe cross R. to Major and Officers. Captain goes up two steps,
stands on platform. As the three Girls cross R., Bebe decides Doctor is
fair game and sits on his lap. Doctor rises indignantly. Harry crosses
R. and apologizes to him, at same time pushes Bebe to R. During this,
Second Officer is trying to converse with Shirley at D.L.C. and Fourth
Officer is similarly engaged with Beulah and Edna at below piano.
When Harry goes to piano with Shirley and Edna, Fourth Officer takes
Beulah into bar L.) And now, while I give some of the girls a lit-
tle rest — I'll slay you with a little specialty of my own. *(During*
above speech Drummer and Violist softly play a hoochie-koochie melody.
All onstage applaud.) Your strict attention is not obligatory!
(Harry sits at piano. Shirley L. of him at piano, Edna R. of him. Sec-
ond Officer sits in chair at Rossi's table at seat D.L. Pittaluga sits L.
end of seat U.C.) My next number will be a little song entitled
"Where have you been all my life — and why didn't you stay
there?" *(Looks significantly at Irene and starts to play the vamp of*
swing music of that period.)
SHIRLEY and EDNA. Yeah, man! Swing it, honey! *(Shirley and*
Edna start snapping their finger and do a little dance to the music.
Dumptsy enters from bar with two buckets filled with champagne bot-

tles, followed by Auguste, bearing six glasses on tray. Dumptsy crosses
R. below and Auguste crosses R. above table at which Irene is sitting.
As they enter Weber rises, excuses himself to Irene, goes up two steps and
talks with Captain. Dumptsy and Auguste serve Officers and Girls at
R. Dumptsy crosses L. below group, exits into bar, returns at once with
bucket of champagne and tray with three glasses, serves Rossis and
Fourth Officer and exits into bar. Quillery, much exited, enters from L.
and arch C., comes D.R. of piano, looks wild-eyed at the gay crowd.)

QUILLERY.   Do you know what has hap-
pened?
DON.   *(Rises, crosses L. to R. of Quillery.)*
I told you we didn't want you here.   *(Spoken together.)*
PITTALUGA. *(Rises, comes D.L. of Quillery.)*
We're having an entertainment here.
QUILLERY.   An entertainment! Yes!
HARRY.   If you'll just sit down, pal ...

QUILLERY.   An entertainment — while Paris is in ruins!
CHERRY.   *(Rises. Crosses L. to L. of Quillery.)* What? What is that
you're saying?
QUILLERY.   They've bombed Paris! The Fascisti have bombed
Paris.

DON.   What? But it can't be possible —
(Harry keeps on playing.)   *(Spoken together.)*
CHERRY.   But how do you know this?

QUILLERY.   It is on the wireless — everywhere. I talked to
one of their mechanics, who was on the flight, and saw, with
his own eyes —
HARRY.   Please sit down, pal. We're trying to give a little entertainment —
QUILLERY.   But tonight — while you sit here laughing and
drinking — *(Harry stops playing piano.)* Italian planes dropped
twenty thousand kilos of bombs on Paris!
CHERRY.   Good God!
QUILLERY.   God knows how many people are killed! God

knows how much of life and beauty is forever destroyed! *(Turns R. toward Officers.)* And you sit here, drinking with *them* — the murderers! *(Breaks away from Don, Pittaluga and Cherry who are holding him and swiftly crosses R. to Officers. Harry rises. Auguste hurriedly crosses L. below Irene's table to below piano.)* They did it. It was their planes from that field down there! *(Cherry swiftly crosses R. to L. of Quillery as Harry rushes R. to Captain, who comes D. from platform threateningly.)*

HARRY. Hey, Captain, speak to your men before anything starts!

SHIRLEY. *(As Harry goes over R.)* Keep out of this, Harry! *(Captain motions Officers, who are muttering, to be still. Don and Pittaluga now cross also to R.)*

QUILLERY. *(To Officers.)* I say, God damn you! Assassins!

MAJOR, FIRST, THIRD OFFICERS and SECOND OFFICER. *(At L. Jump to their feet.)* Assassini!

CAPTAIN. *(Turns R. and commands.)* Si' accomoda! Io mi occupero di lui! Io sono il capo qui!

HARRY. *(As he and Cherry and Don drag Quillery L. across stage.)* Shut up! *(Mrs. Cherry has risen during melee as have the Rossis. Pittaluga stands R. of Mrs. Cherry.)*

QUILLERY. You see, you see, we stand together. France — England — America! ALLIES!

HARRY. Shut up, will you?

QUILLERY. They don't dare fight against the power of England and France! The free democracies against the Fascist tyranny! *(Fourth Officer and Beulah enter from bar, stand below piano.)*

HARRY. Stop fluctuating, will you?

QUILLERY. England and France are fighting for the hopes of mankind!

HARRY. Sure, and a minute ago, England was a butcher in a dress suit. Now we're Allies!

QUILLERY. We stand together.

CHERRY. Yes, I know, but —

QUILLERY. We stand together forever. *(Turns to Officers.)* I say, God damn them. God damn the villains that sent them on their errand of death!

CAPTAIN. *(Takes a few steps L. toward Quillery, slapping his right*

63

boot with his riding crop.) If you don't close your mouth, Frenchman, we shall be forced to arrest you.
QUILLERY.   Go on, Fascisti! Commit national suicide. That's
the last gesture left to you toy soldiers. *(Francine rises, goes to
Major.)*

FRANCINE.   *(Sotto voce.)* What's the   *(Spoken
matter — what's happened?   through other
MAJOR.   *(Gently pushes her aside.)* No, no!   dialogue
(Signals to First and Third Officers, who are R. going on.)*
of him, to keep her quiet.)

HARRY.   It's all right, Captain. Mr. Quillery is for peace. He's
going back to France to stop the war.
QUILLERY.   *(Turns on Harry.)* You're not authorized to speak
for me. I am competent to say what I feel. And what I say is,
(Breaks through Harry and Cherry, who still hold his arms.) "Down
with the Fascisti!" "*Abasso L'Fascisti!*"
CAPTAIN.   *(Ordinarily gentle, is now hot with rage.)* Attenti!
QUILLERY.   *Vive la France!!!* (Harry claps his left hand over
Quillery's mouth.)
CAPTAIN.   *Vi Dichiaro sotto arresto! (To Second Officer at D.L.)
Molinari, Veini con me porco Francese! (Second Officer grabs Quillery
from Harry and Captain grabs Quillery from his end. They take him
U.C. and L. followed by Major and exit. First, Third and Fourth Of-
ficers follow U. to arch C. Rossi collapses from excitement on seat L.)*
BEULAH.   Did he hurt you, Harry?
CHERRY.   *(To Harry.)* You'd better carry on with your turn,
old boy. *(Weber exits in gallery as Quillery is taken out.)*
HARRY.   No, pal, the act is cold. *(Claps his hands to orchestra.)*
Give us some music, signor. Let dancing become general! *(Orchestra starts playing.)*
SHIRLEY.   *(At R. end of piano.)* Come on, get hot! *(Begins
singing the number. Harry picks up his straw hat and swagger stick
and starts to do a dance routine, notices Irene sitting alone at D.R.,
puts hat and stick on piano and crosses R. to her. Officers U. in arch
C., when they see that Quillery is disposed of, come D.: First Officer
crosses R. and dances with Bebe. Third Officer crosses R. and dances*

with Francine. Fourth Officer comes D. to Beulah at below piano and dances with her. Don dances with Edna. Cherry dances with his wife. Doctor sits where he was. Auguste exits hurriedly into bar and returns almost immediately with glass of water, which he gives to Signora Rossi, who in turn tries to revive Rossi as Pittaluga comes D. to them. All above happens simultaneously.)

HARRY.   *(To Irene.)* Would you care to dance?

IRENE.   Why — why, thank you. *(She rises and they dance. The color wheels on both sides of stage now go into action as rest of lights go out.)*

ELAINE.   *(At D.R.)* Hey, Shirley! I'm all alone.

SHIRLEY.   OK. *(She starts to cross R. as curtain falls.)*

CURTAIN

Scene 3

Scene: Later that night.

Everyone seems to have gone to bed. Irene and Harry are alone. She is sitting upstage center of seat upstage center. He is sitting right of her. She is telling the story of her life. He is listening with fascination and doubt. All glasses, bells and ashtrays are struck except on table below center of seat upstage center and ashtray on piano. Table below right end of seat upstage center is stacked on top of table below seat downstage left. Table downstage right is stacked on top of table below steps, and there is a nest of stacked chairs downstage right.

IRENE.   — I was young and strong but — my father was old. The hardships of that terrible journey had broken his body. But his spirit was strong — the spirit that is Russia. He lay there, in that little boat, and he looked up at me. Never can I forget this face, so thin, so white, so beautiful in the starlight. And he said to me, "Irene — little daughter" and then — he died. For four days, I was alone, with his body, in that little boat

65

sailing through the storms of the Black Sea. I had no food — no water — I was in agony from the bayonet wounds of the Botsheviki. I knew I must die. But then — an American cruiser rescued me. May God bless those good men! I've talked too much about myself. What about you, my friend?

HARRY.   Oh — I'm not very interesting. I'm just what I seem to be. *(Looks at her significantly.)*

IRENE.   I do not believe it. *C'est impossible!*

HARRY.   Oh, *c'est possible!* The facts of my case are eloquent. I'm a potential genius — reduced to piloting six blondes through the Balkans.

IRENE.   But there is something that you hide from the world — even, I suspect, from yourself. How did you acquire your superior education?

HARRY.   I worked my way through college selling encyclopaedias.

IRENE.   I knew it! I knew you had culture! What college was it?

HARRY.   Oh — just any college. You know my sales talk was so good I finally fell for it myself and I bought the whole goddamned encyclopaedia. And I read it all.

IRENE.   How did you?

HARRY.   Oh, travelling around, in day coaches, depot hotels, Foxtime dressing rooms. It was worth the money.

IRENE.   And how much of all this have you retained?

HARRY.   *(Significantly.)* I — never forget anything.

IRENE.   Oh, dear, how unfortunate for you! Tell me, does your encyclopaedia help you in your dealings with those young ladies?

HARRY.   Yes, Mrs. Weber ... I get considerable benefit from reading about the great courtesans, and getting to understand their technique ...

IRENE.   Forgive me for interrupting — but that is not my name.

HARRY.   Oh — pardon me, I thought ...

IRENE.   I know — I know what you thought. Monsieur Weber and I are associated in a sort of a — business way.

HARRY.   I see.

IRENE. He does me the honor to consult me in matters of policy.

HARRY. That's quite an honor! Business is pretty good, isn't it?!

IRENE. I gather you are one of those noble souls who do not entirely approve of the munitions industry?

HARRY. No — I'm not noble. Your friend is just another salesman. I make it a point never to criticize anybody else's racket.

IRENE. Monsieur Weber is a very distinguished man. He has rendered very distinguished services to all the governments of the world. For that he has been decorated with the Legion of Honor, the Order of the White Eagle, the Order of St. James of the Sword, the Military Order of Christ —

HARRY. The Military Order of Christ? I never heard of that one.

IRENE. No? Haven't you? Oh, well, it is from Portugal. There are many others.

HARRY. Have you ever been in America?

IRENE. Oh, yes — I have seen it *all* — New York, Washington, Palm Beach!

HARRY. No, I said America. Have you ever been in the West?

IRENE. Certainly. I flew across your continent. There are many White Russians in California.

HARRY. Did you ever happen to make any parachute landings in places like Iowa, or Kansas, or Nebraska?

IRENE. I have seen enough of your countrymen to know that you are typical.

HARRY. *(Coyly.)* Oh, no — oh, no!

IRENE. Oh, yes you are. You are just like all of them — an ingenuous, sentimental idealist. You believe in the goodness of human nature, don't you?

HARRY. Well, what if I do? I've known millions of people, intimately — and I never found more than one out of a hundred that I didn't like, once you got to know them.

IRENE. That is very charming — but it is naive.

HARRY. Maybe so. But experience prevents my working up much enthusiasm over anyone who considers the human race just so many clay pigeons, even if he does belong to the Military Order of Christ.

IRENE.   If you came from an older culture, you would realize that men like Monsieur Weber are necessary to civilization.

HARRY.   Is that so?

IRENE.   I mean the sort of civilization that we have got.

HARRY.   Oh!

IRENE.   People consider him an arch-villain because it is his duty to stir up a little trouble here and there to stimulate the sale of his products. Do you understand me, my friend?

HARRY.   I shouldn't wonder.

IRENE.   He is a true man of the world. He is above petty nationalism; he can be a Frenchman in France — a German in Germany — a Greek — a Turk — whenever the occasion needs it.

HARRY.   Yeah, that little Quillery, he was an Internationalist too. He believed in the brotherhood, but the minute he got a whiff of gunpowder he began to spout hate and revenge. And now I suppose those nice, polite Wops will have to shut him up with a firing squad.

IRENE.   *(Takes cigarette from her case.)* It is a painful necessity.

HARRY.   Well, it just demonstrates the sort of little trouble your friend stirs up. *(He takes out his lighter and lights her cigarette.)*

IRENE.   Do you know you can be extremely rude?

HARRY.   Well, I'm very sorry if I've hurt your feelings about Mr. Weber, but he happens to represent the one percent that I *don't* like.

IRENE.   I was not referring to that. Why do you stare at me so?

HARRY.   Was I staring?

IRENE.   Steadily. Ever since we arrived here this afternoon. Why do you do it?

HARRY.   I was thinking I could notice a funny resemblance to somebody I used to know.

IRENE.   You should know better than to tell a woman that she resembles somebody else. We none of us like to think our appearance is commonplace.

HARRY.   The one you look like wasn't commonplace.

IRENE.   Oh! She was someone near and dear to you?

HARRY.   It was somebody who occupies a unique shrine in the temple of my memory.

IRENE. What a glowing tribute. The temple of your memory — Oh, dear! Well, now I am keeping you from your duties.

HARRY. What duties?

IRENE. Shouldn't you be worrying about those young ladies?

HARRY. They're all right; they've gone to bed.

IRENE. — But there are several Italian officers about. Aren't you the chaperone?

HARRY. I leave the girls to their own resources, of which they have plenty. *(Stares hard at her.)* Were you always a blonde?

IRENE. Yes — as far back as I can remember.

HARRY. You don't mind my asking?

IRENE. No, not at all. And now, may I ask you something?

HARRY. Please do so.

IRENE. Why do you waste yourself in this degraded business? Touring about with those obvious little harlots?

HARRY. You mean you think I'm fitted for something that requires a little more mentality?

IRENE. Oh, yes.

HARRY. How do you know so much about me? *(All through this scene Harry is studying her, trying to fit together the pieces of the jigsaw puzzle of his memory.)*

IRENE. For one thing, I saw your performance tonight.

HARRY. You thought it was punk?

IRENE. No. I thought it was unworthy.

HARRY. It was unfortunately interrupted. If you'd seen the little bit —

IRENE. I saw enough. You are a very bad dancer.

HARRY. The King of Roumania thought I was pretty good.

IRENE. Just the same — my opinion remains unchanged.

HARRY. Well, I'll admit I've done better things. Would it surprise you to know that I was once with a mind-reading act? *(Stares hard at her.)*

IRENE. Really?

HARRY. Yeah.

IRENE. Now, look, you are staring at me like that again.

HARRY. Have you ever been in Omaha?

IRENE. Have I ever been where?

69

HARRY.   In Omaha.

IRENE.   Omaha? Where is that? Persia?

HARRY.   No. Nebraska. That's one of our states.

IRENE.   Really?

HARRY.   I was there once with the greatest act of my career. I was the stooge for Zuleika, the Mind Reader. At least she called me her stooge. But I was the one that did all the brain work. *(Irene laughs.)* But that didn't bother me none.

IRENE.   And she read people's minds?

HARRY.   I did it for her. I passed through the audience and fed her the cues. We were sensational, played the finest picture theatres in the key cities. Zuleika sat on the stage, blindfolded — usually blind drunk.

IRENE.   Oh, dear. And was *she* the one that I resemble?

HARRY.   No! There was another act on the same bill. A troupe of Russians ...

IRENE.   Russians?

HARRY.   — singers, mandolin players, squat dancers. One of them was a red-headed dame. She was fascinated by our act, kept pestering me to teach her the code. She said she could do it better than Zuleika.

IRENE.   Those poor Russians. There are so many of them all over the world. You know that some of them are completely counterfeit.

HARRY.   Yeah, this dame was counterfeit, all right.

IRENE.   She was?

HARRY.   In fact she was the very finest liar I ever met. She kept after me so much that finally I asked her to come up to my room at the hotel one night, and we'd talk it over.

IRENE.   I hope you didn't give her that code.

HARRY.   No. After the week in Omaha the bill split. The Russians went to Sioux Falls, we went on Interstate Time. I played with Zuleika for another year until the drink finally got her and she couldn't retain. So the act busted up. I always hoped I'd meet up with that red-head again sometime. She might have been good. She had the voice for it, and a kind of over-tone of mystery.

IRENE.   It is a characteristic Gypsy quality. And you never saw her again?

HARRY. No!

IRENE. No?

HARRY. No? No!

IRENE. Perhaps it is just as well. She could not have been so very clever — to be duped so easily into coming to your room.

HARRY. She wasn't being duped. She knew what she was doing. If there was any duping going on, she's the one that did it.

IRENE. She did make an impression!

HARRY. *(Looking straight at her.)* I was crazy about her. She was womanhood at its most desirable — and most unreliable.

IRENE. And you such a connoisseur! *(She sighs.)* It is getting very late.

HARRY. *(Rises.)* Do you know any Russian music? *(Crosses L. to piano.)*

IRENE. Oh yes. When I was a little girl my father used to engage Chaliapin to come often to our house. Oh, those were the days! *(Rises.)* He taught me many songs.

HARRY. Chaliapin, eh? My! Your father spared no expense! *(Sits at piano.)*

IRENE. *(Crossing L. toward piano.)* Why should he? That was in *old* Russia! *(Harry starts playing any Russian folksong, perhaps "Kak Stranna."*)* How strange.

HARRY. How very strange! *(Segues into another Russian song.)* Do you know this one? *(Irene Follows music, humming along.)* How do you spell that name — Irene?

IRENE. Ear-ray-na? I-R-E-N-E. *(As she gives him each letter, he punctuates it with a note on piano, going up scale, and when she finishes, he bangs piano and jumps up.)*

HARRY. That's it! Irene! *(He pronounces it I-reen.)*

IRENE. I-reen?

HARRY. I knew it! You're the one!

IRENE. What one?

HARRY. That red-headed liar! Irene! I knew I could never be

---

* See Special Note on Songs and Recordings on copyright page.

mistaken …

IRENE. *(Laughs.)* Ear-ray-na is a very usual name in Russia.

HARRY. I don't care how usual it is. Everything fits together perfectly now. The name — the face — the voice — Chaliapin for a teacher! *(Irene rocks with laughter, shakes her head negatively.)* Certainly it's you! And it's no good shaking your head or trying to look astounded! Because no matter how much you may lie, you can't deny the fact that you slept with me in the Governor Bryan Hotel in Omaha in the fall of 1925. *(Irene laughs heartily again and ad libs, remonstrating. Crosses R. and picks up her purse from table below C. of seat U.C., then crosses L. again.)* Go ahead and laugh. That blond hair had me fooled for a while — but now I know it's just as phoney as the bayonet wounds — parachute jumps into the jungle —

IRENE. *(Still laughing.)* Oh — you amuse me.

HARRY. It's a pleasure to be entertaining. But you can't get away with it.

IRENE. You amuse me very much indeed.

HARRY. Yeah! Ah, ah!

IRENE. Here we are — on a mountain peak in Bedlam. Tonight, the Italians have bombed Paris. At this moment, the French may be bombing Rome, and the English bombing Germany — and the Soviets bombing Tokyo, and all you worry about is whether I am a girl you once met casually in Omaha. *(She crosses R. laughing heartily.)*

HARRY. *(Comes down off platform.)* Did I say it was casual?

IRENE. *(Laughing.)* Oh, you amuse me very much.

HARRY. I admit it's all very amusing. I've admitted a lot of things, tonight, haven't I? I admitted I was crazy about you, didn't I? Well why don't you come across and give me a break?

IRENE. You! So troubled — so uncertain about everything.

HARRY. I'm not uncertain about it any more. *(Passionately.)* Oh — there was something about you that was — indelible … something I couldn't forget all these years. *(Weber appears on gallery, wearing dressing gown and smoking cigar.)*

WEBER. Forgive me for intruding, Irene. But I suggest that it is time for you to go to bed.

IRENE. Yes. Yes, Achille. At once! *(Weber treats Harry to a rather disparaging glance and exits. Irene starts upstairs.)* At once! I am coming. I am coming. Poor Achille! You know, he suffers with the most dreadful insomnia — oh, it is something on his mind. *(At top of stairs.)* He is like Macbeth. Good night, my friend — my funny friend.

HARRY. Good night.

IRENE. Thank you for making me laugh so much — tonight.

HARRY. You know, I could still teach you that code.

IRENE. Perhaps — we shall meet again — in — what was the name of that hotel?

HARRY. The Governor Bryan.

IRENE. Oh, yes! The Governor Bryan! *(Laughing, she exits off gallery. Dumptsy enters from bar, coat off, sleeves rolled up, a large white apron on, and towel in his hand.)*

DUMPTSY. *(At below piano.)* Ach, that was wonderful — that singing and dancing.

HARRY. Thanks, pal. Glad you enjoyed it. *(Picks up straw hat and swagger stick off piano.)*

DUMPTSY. Oh, yes, Mr. Van — that was good.

HARRY. Chaliapin! For God's sake! *(Puts his fist through crown of straw hat, goes U. to arch C.)*

CURTAIN

ACT THREE

Time: The following afternoon.

*Scene: Venetian blinds are up and the waning sun is stream-
ing through windows. Table is back in place as in Act One,
down left below piano. Armchair left of table, side-chair above
table and side-chair right of table. All ashtrays and bells are
struck from all tables. Ashtray on piano still remains. Harry's
overcoat and hat are on right end of seat up center.*

*At rise: Harry, seated at piano smoking a cigarette, is play-
ing an improvised tune. Shirley sits center of seat up center. She
is darning a pair of black silk stockings which are used in the
"number." Bebe stands on platform of first two steps, leaning
against balustrade with a small mirror, and a pair of tweezers, plucking at her eyebrows. Edna is seated seat left below bar
door, writing letters in a portable writing portfolio. At table
down left Beulah, seated in armchair left of table, with cards
laid out on table telling Elaine's fortune. Elaine is seated right
of table. Francine stands above Beulah, watching cards.*

SHIRLEY.   What's that number, Harry?
HARRY.   *(Curtly.)* I don't know.
SHIRLEY.   It's pretty.
HARRY.   You think so? *(Stops playing and puts his cigarette out in
ashtray. Starts to play same number in furious jazz rhythm.)*
BEULAH.   You are going to marry.
ELAINE.   Again?
BEULAH.   The cards indicate *distinctly* two marriages, and
maybe a third.
ELAINE.   *(Chewing furiously.)* For God's sake!
SHIRLEY.   *(To Harry.)* We certainly need some new stockings.
HARRY.   I'm conscious of that.
BEULAH.   Now — let's see what the fates tell us next.

BEBE. Say, Harry — when do we lam it out of here?

HARRY. Ask Beulah. Maybe she can get it out of the cards.

BEULAH. What'd you say, honey?

ELAINE. Ah — don't pay any attention to him.

BEBE. I'll be glad to go. It's kind of spooky around here.

ELAINE. What else do they say about me?

BEULAH. Well, you're going to enter upon a period of very poor health.

ELAINE. When?

BEULAH. Along about your thirty-seventh year.

SHIRLEY. That means any day now.

HARRY. *(Stops playing.)* Listen to me, girls! We can't be wasting our time with card tricks. We've got to do a little rehearsing.

SHIRLEY. Say, Harry — what are you mad about now?

HARRY. Who said I was mad about anything?

SHIRLEY. Well — every time you get yourself into a peeve, you take it out on us. You start hollering "Come on, girls — we got to rehearse."

HARRY. I'm not peeved. Merely a little disgusted. The act needs brushing up.

BEBE. Honestly, Harry — don't you think we know the routine by now?

HARRY. I'm not saying you don't know it. I'm saying your performance last night grieved me and irked me.

FRANCINE. Oh, for God's sake. *(Crosses L., sits above Edna on seat D.L.)*

HARRY. You had your mind on those officers and not on your work. That kind of attitude went big in Roumania, but now we're going to a town where artistry counts. Some day I'll take the bunch of you to see the Russian ballet, give you a rough idea of what dancing really is.

CAPTAIN. *(Enters from L. and arch C.)* Your pardon, Mr. Van.

EDNA, FRANCINE, BEULAH and BEBE. *(Girls rise and Bebe comes down from platform at R. Crosses L. to R. end of seat U.C.)* Good afternoon, Captain.

HARRY. Rest, girls, rest. *(Comes down from platform. Edna, Francine and Beulah sit as before. To Captain.)* Any news?

CAPTAIN. Good news, I hope. May I have your passports?

HARRY. Yes, certainly. *(Crosses R. below Captain toward his coat, as Bebe gets passports out of pocket of his coat and gives them to Harry.)*
CAPTAIN. *(Crosses R. to Harry.)* I hope to have definite word for you very shortly.
HARRY. Oh, thanks. *(Harry gives him passports.)*
CAPTAIN. Thank you. *(Salutes and starts to go U.C.)*
HARRY. What happened to Mr. Quillery?
CAPTAIN. Mr. Quillery was very injudicious. Very injudicious. I am glad that you are so much more intelligent. *(Salutes and goes out C. and L.)*
SHIRLEY. Oh, I don't think they could have done anything cruel to him. They're awfully nice boys, those Wops.
HARRY. *(At R.)* Yeah, so I observed … Now listen to me, girls. *(Crosses L. to C.)* Geneva's big time, and we've got to be good. You know your audiences aren't going to be a lot of hunkies, who don't care what you do as long as you don't wear practically any pants. These people are big shots. They're mains — they're used to the best, they're like prime ministers, maharajahs, archbishops. If we click with them, we're all set for London and Paris. Maybe we'll even get enough money to get home.
BEBE. *(Sitting at R. end of seat U.C.)* Oh — don't speak of such a thing! Home!
HARRY. The trouble with you girls is, you're thinking too much about your own specialties. You're trying to steal the act, and you wreck it. Remember what the late Knute Rockne said: "Somebody else can have the all-star, all-American aggregations. All *I* ask is a team!" *(Comes D. to above Beulah.)* Now, you — Beulah. You've got plenty of chance to score individually in your bubble number. But when you come to the chorus routine, you've got to submerge your genius to the mass.
BEULAH. What do I do wrong?
HARRY. What do you do wrong? Your Maxie Ford is lackluster. *(He demonstrates it.)*
SHIRLEY. *(Laughs, rises, comes D.R. of Harry.)* Come here, Beulah — *I'll* show you.
HARRY. Just a minute, Miss Laughlin. Who's directing this act, you or me?

SHIRLEY. *(Good-naturedly slaps his face.)*
You are, you old poop. But you just don't
know the steps. *(Spoken*
ELAINE. Don't let her get fresh, Harry. *together.)*
BEBE. Slap her down!
SHIRLEY. Give us the music, Harry.

BEULAH. *(Rises, crosses R. to Harry.)* Please, Harry. Shirley just
wants to be helpful.
HARRY. *(Goes U. to piano.)* I feel I ought to resent this.
SHIRLEY. Don't be silly. Give us a pick-up. *(Harry sits at piano,
starts to play chorus "Putting on the Ritz."* Francine rises, crosses R.
and sits chair L. of table D.L. and lays out cards. Edna rises and
crosses R., stands above Francine. Bebe rises, crosses L. and stands
above table D.L. Shirley and Beulah are doing the number. During this
following conversation goes on.)*
ELAINE. *(Still seated chair R. of table D.L.)* You know that Wop
was giving me a play last night?
FRANCINE. You mean the one with the bent nose?
ELAINE. I thought he was terrible. But the boy I had is a
Count.
SHIRLEY. *(Finishing her demonstration to Beulah.)* Get it? *(Harry
keeps on playing. Beulah goes U., sits at L. end of seat U.C., Shirley
comes D. to above group at table D.L.)*
ELAINE. *(Taking out a coin.)* Well, look what he gave me.
EDNA. What is it?
BEBE. Let me see it.
ELAINE. I don't know what it is.
BEBE. *(Takes coin.)* Looks like money. *(Goes U. to piano, followed
by other Girls in group.)* What kind of money is this, Harry?
HARRY. What? *(Stops playing.)*
BEBE. What kind of money is this?
HARRY. *(Looks at it.)* That's an old Roman coin.
SHIRLEY. How much is it worth?
HARRY. I haven't looked up the latest rate of exchange on
diners — but, dear, I'm afraid you've been betrayed. *(Bebe gives*

* See Special Note on Songs and Recordings on copyright page.

77

Elaine the coin. Edna goes U. and sits above Beulah on seat U.C.) Now listen to me, girls, pay attention. I said the act needed improving, and with that in mind ... *(He rises.)* I'm going to retire from all dance routines.

BEBE.   What?

ELAINE. *(At R. end of piano.)* Why, Harry.	*(Spoken together.)*
BEULAH. Why, Harry, we couldn't get along without you. *(Francine rises, goes U.L. end of piano, Bebe goes U.L. of Harry on platform.)*	

SHIRLEY.   *(R. of Harry on platform.)* Why, Harry, I hurt you, didn't I! I'm sorry. I didn't mean it.

HARRY.   Never mind the regrets, Shirley.

SHIRLEY.   Give me a kiss.

HARRY.   Save your lipstick.

SHIRLEY.   But why do you want to do that?

HARRY.   I've decided I'm more of a thinker than a performer. From now on I shall devote myself purely to the creative side of the act, and of course, negotiate all contracts. *(He sits.)*

FRANCINE. What the hell is the matter with you? Have you gone screwy?	*(Spoken together.)*
BEBE. When did you make up your mind to that, Harry?	

HARRY.   I've been considering this for some time.

SHIRLEY.   Say! What were you talking about to that Russian dame?

HARRY.   We discussed world politics.

FRANCINE.   Oh!

SHIRLEY.   *(Her elbow on Harry's right shoulder, chin on her hand.)* Oh! And how are politics these days?

BEBE.   Harry, did you get anywhere near first base?

HARRY.   I find it very difficult to explain certain things to you girls. You're children of nature.

SHIRLEY.   We're *what?*

BEULAH.   He means we're natural.

SHIRLEY.   Oh.

HARRY.   *(To Beulah.)* Oh, God! Never mind, sweetheart. *(To Shirley.)* You'll sing the number, Shirley.

SHIRLEY.   *(Pleased.)* Me?

BEBE.   With that terrible voice? *(Francine comes D., sits chair R. of table.)*

HARRY.   *(To Bebe.)* She handled it fine that time I had bronchitis in Belgrade. And with a little rehearsing ... *(Turns to Shirley.)* you'll have the whole League of Nations rooting for you. Come on, now! *(Starts playing the verse of "Putting on the Ritz."* Elaine crosses R., sits R. of Beulah on seat U.C. Shirley starts singing. Bebe holds her nose in contempt.)* Ah, scram! Take it again, Harry. *(Harry begins verse again. Bebe gets off platform, crosses R.: As she passes Shirley, Shirley tries to kick her in the behind. Bebe crosses R. to R. end of seat U.C.)*

HARRY.   That's fine! *(Don enters from L. and C. arch, hat and overcoat on. Comes D., and stops at R. corner of piano.)*

BEULAH and FRANCINE.   Hello, Don.

DON.   *(Takes hat off.)* Hello — Say, Harry, Captain Locicero has got the orders to let us through and the train leaves at five o'clock. *(Crosses R. below group.)*

GIRLS.   *(Ad lib.)* Hooray!

DON.   What a relief to be out of this foul place! *(Goes up steps. Shirley gets off platform, crosses R. to below seat U.C.)*

HARRY.   *(Still playing.)* You going, too, Don?

DON.   Yes. There's nothing for me here. As a matter of fact, I'm sick of Europe as a whole. *(At top of stairs.)* I was in town this morning when they shot Quillery. *(Harry stops playing.)*

BEBE.   *(Looking up at Don.)* Shot who?

SHIRLEY.   That little guy that bawled out the Wops.

BEULAH.   *(Looking up at Don.)* They *shot* him? Why did they have to do that?

DON.   Well, he asked for it. But even so, it's pretty sickening to see one of your fellow human beings crumpled up in violent death. There'll be lots more like him, and right here, too. The

* See Special Note on Songs and Recordings on copyright page.

French know about this air base, and pretty soon they'll be over with their bombs. So — it's California here I come! *(Starts to go.)*

HARRY.   Yeah, and bump right into the Japs? You'd better stop off at Wichita.

DON.   I'll see you on the train. *(Goes out.)*

HARRY.   You girls go get yourselves ready.

ELAINE.   OK, Harry *(She starts for arch C., goes out R.)*

FRANCINE.   *(Rises, takes cards with her.)* Hey! Let's see that coin again.

EDNA.   Maybe you can pass it off in a slot machine. *(Exits U.C. and R.)* I just love to hear those Wops talk. They make everything sound like opera.

FRANCINE.   I'll say!

BEULAH.   *(Rises. Crosses L. to piano. To Harry.)* But I can't understand … why did they have to shoot the poor boy? *(Shirley is getting her sewing box together.)*

HARRY.   Well, it's hard to explain, Beulah. But it seems they're having an argument over here, and the only way they care to settle it is by murdering a lot of people. *(The Cherrys appear on gallery, all dressed for travelling, as in Act One, and come D. Cherry is carrying Mrs. Cherry's coat on his arm.)*

SHIRLEY.   *(Crosses L. to R. of Beulah.)* Say — you don't need to tell me what that's like. I was in the Club Grotto in Detroit the night the Purple Gang shot it out with the Gs. *(She and Beulah start out U.C.)* And was that terrible! Blood all over everything! You never saw such a mess. *(They exit R.)*

HARRY.   *(To Cherry at C.)* Well, you heard what happened to Quillery?

CHERRY.   Yes. It seems he died like a true patriot, shouting "*Vive la France.*"

HARRY.   Been better if he died like a man — sticking to what he thought was right.

CHERRY.   He was such a nice little chap.

MRS. CHERRY.   *(Comes down two steps from platform, crosses L. to Cherry.)* The Italians are swine! *(Don enters on gallery with bag and portable Victoria, comes downstairs. Crosses L. below Cherrys.)*

CHERRY.   Oh, they had a perfect right to do it.

MRS. CHERRY.   I know, darling, but to kill a man just for saying what he thinks!

CHERRY.   Many people will be killed for less than that.

HARRY.   *(Rises, comes down off platform.)* I'll have to be saying good-bye pretty soon. *(To Don.)* The train does leave at five? Doesn't it?

DON.   Yeah. Five o'clock sharp. *(Exits arch C. and L.)*

HARRY.   I hope all this unpleasantness hasn't spoiled your winter sports. *(Mrs. Cherry turns away R., crosses R. a few steps.)*

CHERRY.   Oh, that's all washed up. We're going back, too — that is if they'll let us cross the border.

HARRY.   So the honeymoon is over already?

MRS. CHERRY.   *(On verge of tears.)* Yes — I suppose so.

CHERRY.   England's coming into this. We've got to stand by France, of course. And so — *(Goes U.C. of seat U.C.)*

MRS. CHERRY.   And so Jimmy will have to do his bit, manning the guns for civilization. *(Cherry sits seat U.C., Harry crosses R. below Cherry to R. of him, picks up hat off table R. end of seat U.C., and his coat off seat U.C.)* Perhaps he'll join in the bombardment of Florence, where we were married!

CHERRY.   You know — after the ceremony we went into the Baptistery and we prayed to the soul of Leonardo da Vinci that we might never fail in our devotion to that which was beautiful and true. I told you we were a bit on the romantic side. Well, we forgot what Leonardo said about war. Bestial frenzy, he called it. And bestial frenzy it is.

MRS. CHERRY.   Yes, but we mustn't think about that now. We have to stand by France. We have to make the world a decent place for heroes to live in. *(Breaks, begins to sob.)* Oh, Christ!

CHERRY.   *(Quickly rises, crosses R. below Harry to her.)* We've got to make the best of it. Now, darling, please don't cry!

HARRY.   *(Crosses R. to C., hat and coat in hand.)* Let her cry, let her sob her heart out — for all the good it will do her. You know what I often think? I often think we ought to get together and elect somebody else God. Yeah, me for instance. I'd bet I'd make a much better job of it!

MRS. CHERRY. *(Through tears.)* You'd be fine, Mr. Van.

HARRY. I think I would at that. There'd be a lot of people object to my methods. That Mr. Weber, for instance. Would I begin the administration by beating the can off-a him!

CHERRY. Let's start the campaign now! Vote for good old Harry Van, and his Three Angels! *(Captain enters from L. and U.C. with briefcase full of papers and passports. Comes D. to R. of Harry.)*

CAPTAIN. Good afternoon, Mrs. Cherry. Gentlemen.

HARRY. Well, do we get across?

CAPTAIN. Here is your passport, Mr. Van — and the young ladies', with my compliments. They have been duly stamped. *(Hands them over, crosses L. below Harry to table D.L.)*

HARRY. How about Mr. Weber and his — friend? Do they go, too?

CAPTAIN. I have their passports here. I advise you to make ready, Mr. Van. *(Puts hat and gloves on chair above table D.L. Looks at wristwatch.)* The train will leave in about forty-five minutes. *(He opens briefcase on table and sits chair L. of table.)*

HARRY. OK, Captain. See you later, Mr. and Mrs. Cherry. *(Goes out C. and R.)*

CHERRY. OK, Harry.

MRS. CHERRY. *(Curtly.)* What about us?

CAPTAIN. Due to a slight technicality, you will be permitted to cross the frontier. Here are your passports.

CHERRY. *(Crosses L. to table D.L., followed by Mrs. Cherry, and takes passports.)* I can't tell you how grateful we are.

CAPTAIN. You needn't be grateful to me, Mr. Cherry. The fact that you're allowed to pass is due to the superb centralization of authority in my country. The telegram authorizing your release was filed at 11:43 today, just seventeen minutes before a state of war was declared between Great Britain and Italy. I must obey the order of Rome, even though I know it's out of date. Is your luggage ready?

CHERRY. Yes, it's all out in the hall. Well, good-bye and good luck!

CAPTAIN. *(Rises.)* And good luck to you — both of you

CHERRY. I need hardly say how terribly sorry we are about

all this. It's really a damned rotten shame.

CAPTAIN.   It is. All of that. Good-bye, my friend. *(Extends hand and Cherry shakes it, then extends hand to Mrs. Cherry.)*

CHERRY.   Good-bye.

MRS. CHERRY.   Don't you call *me* your friend, because I say what Quillery said, damn you — damn your whole country of mad dogs for having started this horror. *(Weber appears on gallery, his overcoat and hat on and carrying leather portfolio.)*

CAPTAIN.   *(Bows.)* It is not my fault, Mrs. Cherry.

CHERRY.   It's utterly unfair to talk that way, darling. The Captain is doing his miserable duty as decently as he possibly can. Now, please, darling.

MRS. CHERRY.   I know ... I know. Forgive me.

CAPTAIN.   Madame!

MRS. CHERRY.   *(Extends hand to Captain, shakes hands.)* I should have remembered that it's everybody's fault. *(To Cherry.)* Oh, I'll be all right, Jimmy.

CHERRY.   Come on, my sweet. *(They exit U.C. and L.)*

CAPTAIN.   *(To Weber.)* Frankly, my heart bleeds for them. *(Sits.)*

WEBER.   They're young. They'll live through it, and be happy. *(Starts to come D., crosses L. to Captain during Captain's speech.)*

CAPTAIN.   Will they? I was their age, and in their situation, twenty years ago, when I was sent to the Isonzo front. And people said just that to me: "Never mind — you are young — and youth will survive and come to triumph." And I believed it. That is why I couldn't say such deceiving words to them now.

WEBER.   The civilization of hope never does any immediate harm. Is everything ready?

CAPTAIN.   *(Rises.)* Quite! Monsieur Weber. Here it is. *(Hands over Weber's passport. Five of the Girls and Harry cross from R. to L. at back in arch. They have on coats and hats and carry their luggage, etc. Harry carries his briefcase.)*

SHIRLEY.   I'm certainly glad to get out of this joint.

BEBE.   So long, Captain.

ELAINE.   Have you got the music, Harry?

HARRY.   Yeah. I got it. Have you got your overshoes?

FRANCINE.   *(To Captain.)* Toodle-doo, Captain.

EDNA.   See you in church, Cap. *(They disappear in passageway.)*

WEBER.   And Madame's?

CAPTAIN.   *(Holds up Irene's passport.)* Madame's passport is quite unusual, Monsieur Weber. It has given us some worry.

WEBER.   The League of Nations issues documents like that to those whose nationality is uncertain.

CAPTAIN.   I understand — but the attitude of Italy toward the League of Nations is not at the moment cordial. So the authorities insist that I ask some questions — as a mere matter of formality.

WEBER.   You may ask questions, Captain, but you can be sure of none of the answers. All that I know is that her father was an Armenian, who got into trouble with the Tsarist government in Russia. I believe he was a thrower of bombs.

CAPTAIN.   Does Madame inherit any of his tendencies?

WEBER.   I shouldn't wonder. But she has learned to control them.

CAPTAIN.   Very well, Monsieur Weber. My instructions are to accord you every consideration. In view of the fact that Madame is travelling with you, I shall be glad to approve her visa. *(Sits.)*

WEBER.   Madame is not travelling with me. She has her own passport.

CAPTAIN.   But it is understood that you vouch for her, and that is enough to satisfy the authorities.

WEBER.   Vouch for her? It is not necessary for anybody to vouch for Madame! She is quite capable of taking care of herself. If her passport is not entirely in order, it is no affair of mine.

CAPTAIN.   Monsieur Weber, I must tell you that this is something which I do not like. This places me in a — most embarrassing position. I shall be forced to detain Madame.

WEBER.   You are a soldier, Captain, and you should be used to embarrassing positions. Undoubtedly, you were embarrassed this morning when you had to shoot that confused pacifist, Quillery. But this is war, and distasteful responsibilities descend upon you as well as on me.

HARRY.   *(Yells, off L. of arch.)* Beulah! *(Appears in arch C.)*

BEULAH.   *(Yells, off R. of arch.)* Yes, Harry.

HARRY. They're waiting for you in the bus.

BEULAH. I'm coming. *(Crosses from R. to L. in arch, hat and coat on.)*

HARRY. Tell them I'll be right out. *(Beulah, carrying luggage, disappears in hall at L. Harry comes D.)*

BEULAH. OK, Harry. *(Doctor appears on gallery with coat, hat, books done in a bundle and umbrella. He has his overshoes on. Comes downstairs.)*

WEBER. I shall attend to my luggage. Thank you, Captain. *(Exits U. arch C. and L.)*

CAPTAIN. Don't mention it. *(To Harry.)* The young ladies are ready?

HARRY. Yes — they're ready. And some of your aviators are out there trying to persuade them into staying here permanently.

CAPTAIN. *(Smiling.)* And I add my entreaties to theirs.

HARRY. We aren't going to have any more trouble, are we?

CAPTAIN. Oh, no, Mr. Van. Geneva is a lovely spot. All of Switzerland is beautiful these days. I envy you going there, in such charming company.

HARRY. *(Puts coat and hat on L. end of seat U.C., then sits.)* Hi, Doctor. Got your rats all packed?

DOCTOR. Good afternoon. I am privileged to go now? *(Puts all his belongings R. end of seat U.C. and overcoat on table R. end of seat U.C.)*

CAPTAIN. Yes, Dr. Waldersee. Here is your passport.

DOCTOR. Thank you. *(Doctor crosses L. to chair R. of table D.L. and sits and takes out eyeglass case, puts on eyeglasses and examines passports carefully.)*

HARRY. *(Rises, comes D. to above table D.L.)* I can tell you this, Doctor — I certainly will be proud to have known you. When I read in the papers that you've wiped out cancer and won the Nobel prize, and are one of the greatest heroes on earth, I'll be able to say: "He was a personal friend of mine." *(Nudges Captain, who chuckles.)* He once admired my music.

DOCTOR. *(Solemnly, to Harry.)* Thank you very much. *(To Captain.)* This visa is good for crossing the Austrian border!

CAPTAIN. Certainly. But you are going to Zurich!

DOCTOR. *(Puts eyeglasses in case, then in vest pocket.)* I have changed my plans. I'm going back into Germany. *(Rises.)* Germany is at war. Perhaps I am needed. *(Crosses R., picks up overcoat.)*

HARRY. Needed for what?

DOCTOR. I shall offer my services for what they are worth.

HARRY. *(Crosses R., helps Doctor put on coat.)* But what about the rats?

DOCTOR. Why should I save people who don't want to be saved — so they can go out and exterminate each other? Obscene maniacs! *(Starts to put on gloves.)* Then I'll be a maniac, too. I'll be more dangerous than most of them. I know all the tricks of death! As for my rats, maybe they'll be useful. Britain will put down the blockade again, and we shall be starving. — Maybe I'll cut up my rats into fillets and eat them. *(Goes U. and gets hat, books and umbrella from seat U.C.)*

HARRY. Wait a minute, Doctor. You're doing this without thinking ...

DOCTOR. I'm thinking — probably the remedy you sold is better than mine. Hasten to apply it. We're all diseased.

HARRY. But you can't change around like this! Don't you remember all those things you told me? All that about back-sliding?

DOCTOR. No, I have not forgotten the degradation of mankind — *(Crosses L. above Harry and U.C.)* that is painful and offensive to conceive. *(In arch C.)* I'm sorry to disappoint you about the Nobel Prize! *(Grunts, exits to L.)*

HARRY. Good-bye, Doctor! *(Sits on L. end of seat U.C., speaks to Captain, with uncharacteristic vehemence.)* Why can't somebody answer the question everybody asks? Why!! I know some of the answers — but then they aren't good enough. Weber — and a lot like him — they can't take the blame for *all* of this. Who is it did this trick on a lot of decent people? And why do you let 'em get away with it? That's the thing I'd like to know!

CAPTAIN. We have avalanches up here, my friend. They are disastrous. They start with a little crack in the ice, so tiny that one can hardly see it — until — suddenly — it bursts wide open. And then it is too late!

86

HARRY. That's all very well. But it doesn't satisfy me — because this avalanche isn't made of ice. *(Irene appears on gallery all dressed for travelling. She is putting on her gloves as she comes downstairs.)* It's made of flesh and blood — and — *brains!*
IRENE. Still worrying about the situation, Mr. Van? *(Lights begin to dim slowly.)* Good afternoon, Captain Locicero.
CAPTAIN. *(Rises.)* Good afternoon, Madame. *(Harry rises, too.)*
IRENE. I have had the most superb rest here. It is so calm, so soothing. I can't bear to think that I have to go to Biarritz. *(Weber enters from L. and arch C., comes D. to L. of Harry.)* With the dull, dismal old sea pounding in my ears. We are ready now, Achille?
WEBER. *(Takes off hat.)* The — Captain has raised some objections. *(Looks at Captain significantly.)*
CAPTAIN. I regret, Madame, that there must be some further delay.
IRENE. The train is not going, after all?
CAPTAIN. The train is going, Madame. But this passport of yours presents problems which, under the circumstances —
IRENE. *(Crosses L. to C.)* Monsieur Weber will settle them, whatever the problems are. Won't you, Achille?
WEBER. I have just been arguing with the Captain. There is some difficulty about your nationality.
CAPTAIN. *(Looking at passport.)* Your birthplace is uncertain, Madame — believed to be in Armenia.
IRENE. Yes — a province of Russia —
CAPTAIN. You subsequently became a resident of England —
IRENE. When I was a very little girl.
CAPTAIN. — Then you went to the United States — and then to France — *(Harry sits again on L. end of seat U.C.)*
IRENE. Yes, yes — it is all there — plain for you to see — *(Crosses L. to chair R. of table D.L.)* I have never had the slightest difficulty about my passport. It was issued by the League of Nations. *(Sits chair R. of table.)*
WEBER. *(Gives Captain the eye.)* I'm afraid that the standing of the League of Nations is not very high in Italy at this moment.
CAPTAIN. *(Taking his cue from Weber.)* The fact is, Madame, the very existence of the League is no longer recognized by our

government. For that reason, we cannot permit you to cross the frontier at this time. *(Significantly, to Irene.)* I'm sure you will appreciate the *delicacy* of my position. *(Hands her passport over table. Picks up hat and briefcase.)* Perhaps we shall be able to adjust the matter — tomorrow. *(Puts hat on, clicks heels and salutes, crosses U. above Weber. Harry rises, takes Captain by sleeve and pantomimes he would like to know why Irene can't get out. They exit U.C. arch and L.)*

WEBER.   *(Sits chair above table D.L., puts hat on table.)* I should of course wait over, Irene. But you know how dangerous it is for me to delay my return to France by so much as one day. I have been in touch with our agents. The Premier is demanding that production be doubled — trebled — at once.

IRENE.   I understand, Achille.

WEBER.   Here — *(Takes out envelope from overcoat pocket.)* this will take care of all possible expenses. *(Gives it to her.)* You must return to Venice immediately and see Lanza. I have already sent him full instructions.

IRENE.   Thank you for being so very tactful.

WEBER.   *(Rises, puts chair in place close to table.)* You're a superior person, Irene. I consider it a great privilege to have known you.

IRENE.   Thank you, again.

WEBER.   Good-bye, my dear. *(He goes to kiss her.)*

IRENE.   *(Offers him her hand to shake, instead.)* Good-bye, good-bye, Achille. *(Weber shakes her hand, turns U.C. and starts to go U. as Harry reenters from L. and arch C.)*

WEBER.   Coming, Mr. Van? *(Exits U.C. arch and L.)*

HARRY.   Yeah, certainly. *(Comes D. as Irene puts envelope in her handbag to chair L. of table D.L.)* Tough luck, babe.

IRENE.   It is no matter.

HARRY.   *(Sits chair L. of table.)* But I seriously doubt you'll suffer any bayonet wounds. You know, the Captain isn't as brutal as the Bolsheviks were.

IRENE.   You mean to be encouraging.

HARRY.   *(Notices her passport on table.)* How did you get that passport from the League of Nations?

IRENE.   I am under oath not to say anything about that. *(She*

starts to pick it up.)
HARRY.   *(Reaches for* it.) Let me see it.
IRENE.   No!
HARRY.   I want to see it. Give it to me.
IRENE.   Don't you dare touch it! *(Harry snatches it from her. Shirley appears in arch C. from L.)*
SHIRLEY.   Hey, Harry. It's time for us to go! *(Harry looks up at Shirley.)*
HARRY.   All right, all right. *(He is looking at passport. Shirley goes.)*
IRENE.   Go away with your friends.
HARRY.   *(Reading.)* "Irene Kasmadjians" — Kasmadjians. Is that a branch of the Romanoffs, babe?
IRENE,   Don't call me *babe!* *(Takes passport from him, puts it in her handbag.)*
HARRY.   My apologies, Madame. I just call everybody "babe."
IRENE.   Perhaps that is why I don't like it. *(Rises, crosses R.)*
HARRY.   *(Rises, crosses to her.)* I can see that you're in a tough spot. And considering what we were to each other in the old Governor Bryan Hotel —
IRENE.   Must you always be in that place?
HARRY.   I want to help you, Irene. Isn't there something I can do?
IRENE.   I thank you, from the bottom of my heart, I thank you for that offer. But it is useless ...
HARRY.   Listen, you don't have to thank me. Just tell me — what can I do?
IRENE.   You're very kind, and very gallant. But unfortunately, you're no match for Achille Weber.
HARRY.   Is he responsible for them stopping you?
IRENE.   Of course he is. *(Crosses L. below Harry.)* I knew it the moment I saw that ashamed look on the face of Captain Locicero, when he refused to permit me —
HARRY.   *(Crosses L. to her.)* So Weber double-crossed you, did he? Well, what's that son-of-a-bitch got against you?
IRENE.   He's afraid of me. *(Crosses R. below Harry.)* I know too much about him and his methods of promoting his own business.
HARRY.   *(Crosses R. to bar.)* Everybody knows about his meth-

ods. Even little Quillery was talking about them last night —

IRENE.   And what happened to Quillery? It is what happens to everyone who dares to criticize them.

HARRY.   Why? Did you split with him?

IRENE.   Yes. Last night I could stand it no longer. So I did the one thing I knew he never would forgive.

HARRY.   Yeah?

IRENE.   I told him what I really thought about his business!

HARRY.   *(Jubilant.)* Yeah? *(Shirley and Bebe appear in arch C. from L.)*

IRENE.   See how quickly he strikes back.

SHIRLEY.   Harry! The bus is going to leave!

HARRY.   *(To Shirley.)* All right — all right!

BEBE.   *(Shouts as they go L.)* But we gotta go right this minute.

IRENE.   Go along, go along. You can't help me now. Nobody can.

SHIRLEY and IRENE.   *(Offstage, yelling.)* Harry!

IRENE.   You will miss your train.

HARRY.   All right! *(Gets coat, hat and briefcase from seat U.C.)*

IRENE.   But if it will make you any happier in your travels with Les Blondes I will tell you: I did know you — slightly — in Omaha.

HARRY.   Are you lying again?

IRENE.   It was room 974.

HARRY.   Well how the hell can I remember what room it was?

IRENE.   Well then — you'll never be sure, Mr. Van.

DON.   *(Appears in L. end of arch C.)* Will you come on? We can't wait another instant! *(Goes out again L.)*

HARRY.   *(Starts for arch C.)* Yeah, I'm coming.

DON.   *(Off.)* Hurry up, you can put your coat on in the bus.

HARRY.   I said I'm coming, goddamn it. Can't you hear me? *(Goes out arch C. and L. Irene, left alone, goes to R. end of seat U.C., takes off her gloves, puts handbag on seat, takes off cloak, puts it on table below R. end of seat, takes off hat, puts it on top of cloak, and with a sigh, sits extreme R. end of seat U.C. Dumptsy enters from arch C. and L., wearing uniform of a private in the Italian Alpini corps, a full pack on his back.)*

DUMPTSY.   Oh, good afternoon, Madame.

IRENE. Why, Dumptsy — what is that costume?

DUMPTSY. They called me up. Look! I'm an Italian soldier.

IRENE. You look splendid!

DUMPTSY. If you please, Madame. But why did you not go on that bus, Madame?

IRENE. I have decided to remain here and enjoy the winter sports.

DUMPTSY. Oh, I don't think this is a good place any more, Madame. They say the war is very big — bigger than last time.

IRENE. I heard that too.

DUMPTSY. The French will be here to drop bombs on everybody.

IRENE. That will be very exciting for us if they do, won't it?

DUMPTSY. It is possible, Madame. But ... I came to say goodbye to Auguste, the barman, and Anna, the maid. They're both cousins of mine. They'll laugh when they see me in these clothes. *(He goes to L.)* Can I get you anything, Madame? — *(Pittaluga enters from L., appears in arch C.)*

IRENE. Yes, Dumptsy. Bring me a *(Pittaluga pushes light switch on back wall of hall of arch, lights up room.)* bottle of champagne ... bring two glasses ... we'll have a drink together.

DUMPTSY. If you please, Madame. *(Goes into bar. Pittaluga enters from arch C., comes D. to L. of her.)*

PITTALUGA. Your luggage is in the hall, Madame. Will you wish it taken to the same suite?

IRENE. No — I didn't really care for those rooms. Have you something a little smaller?

PITTALUGA. We have smaller rooms on the other side of the hotel.

IRENE. I will have the smallest. It will be cozier. *(Dumptsy returns with champagne and two white champagne glasses on tray.)*

PITTALUGA. You wish to go to it now?

IRENE. No. Have my luggage sent up. I'll see it later. *(Pittaluga bows, goes U.C, exits.)*

DUMPTSY. *(Puts tray on table below C. of seat U.C.)* I was right, Madame. Auguste laughed very much.

IRENE. What will become of your wife and children, Dumptsy?

DUMPTSY. Oh — I suppose the Fascisti will feed them. They

91

promised to feed all the families with a man out fighting for their country. *(He has filled her glass and gives it to her.)*

IRENE.   So? Pour yourself one.

DUMPTSY.   Thank you so much, Madame. I was not sure I heard correctly. *(Pours for himself.)*

IRENE.   *(Holds up glass.)* To you, Dumptsy — and to Austria.

DUMPTSY.   And to you, Madame, if you please. *(Clinks her glass.)*

IRENE.   Thank you. *(They drink.)*

DUMPTSY.   *(Smacks lips.)* This is good. And may you soon be restored to your home in Petersburg.

IRENE.   My home — huh! *(Holds up her glass.)* No fear ...

DUMPTSY.   No, Madame — *(They clink their glasses and drink.)* And now I must go find Anna, if you please. *(Starts L.)*

IRENE.   *(Rises.)* One moment. Here. *(Digs into handbag, hands him note of money.)* For you —

DUMPTSY.   Thank you so much, Madame.

IRENE.   Good-bye, Dumptsy, and may God bless you. *(Offers her hand.)*

DUMPTSY.   Kiss *die hand*, Madame. *(Leans over, kisses her hand. Major and Captain come in from L. and U.C., talking.)*

MAJOR.   *Non ce molto temp, Signor Capitano.*

CAPTAIN.   *E allora, Signor Maggiori. Beviamo prima e dopo andiamo al campo d'avione. (Dumptsy salutes strenuously and exits U.C. and L. Major crosses L. and into bar. Captain is following him.)*

IRENE.   Some champagne, Captain?

CAPTAIN.   No, thank you very much, Madame.

IRENE.   You need not be so anxious to avoid me. I know perfectly well it was not your fault.

CAPTAIN.   *(Takes off hat.)* You are very understanding, Madame.

IRENE.   That is true. I am the most understanding woman in this world. I understand so damned much that I am alone on this cold mountain peak, and I have no one to turn to ... and nowhere to go ...

CAPTAIN.   If I can be of service to you, Madame, in any way ...

IRENE.   *(Crosses L. to C.)* I know, you'll be very kind and faultlessly polite.

CAPTAIN. I realize, Madame, that politeness now means nothing. But under these tragic circumstances, what else can I do?
IRENE. What else can you do under these tragic circumstances? I will tell you what you can do. You are a man, you can refuse to fight — you can refuse to use those weapons they have sold you. *(Goes U. to piano, champagne glass in hand, as Captain backs U.L. toward her.)* But you were going into the bar. Don't let me detain you.
CAPTAIN. You will forgive me, Madame?
IRENE. Fully, my dear Captain, fully.
CAPTAIN. Thank you, Madame. Thank you very much. *(Salutes and goes into bar. Irene sits at piano and plays with one finger a few notes of a Russian song of the period, then segues into a Cockney song of the period and sings. Harry enters from L. through arch C. with hat and overcoat on, carrying briefcase and Gladstone bag. Puts bag on floor below seat U.C. and briefcase on seat. Irene rises.)* Did you have some trouble?
HARRY. *(Takes off coat and hat and puts them on briefcase.)* No. Whose champagne is that?
IRENE. Mine. Will you have some?
HARRY. Thanks. *(Starts to pour it in Dumptsy's glass.)*
IRENE. Dumptsy used that glass.
HARRY. *(His back to her.)* That's all right. *(Fills glass.)*
IRENE. Did you miss your train?
HARRY. No. The train went. I got the girls on board. Mr. and Mrs. Cherry promised to look after them. They'll be OK. *(Drinks.)*
IRENE. And you have come back here to me?
HARRY. It seems perfectly obvious I came back.
IRENE. Then you meant it when you said you wanted to help me.
HARRY. *(Turns L. to her.)* You said I'd never be sure. Well, I came back to tell you that I *am* sure. I got thinking back, in that bus, and I came to the conclusion that it *was* room 974 — or close to it, anyhow. And somehow or other, I couldn't help feeling a little flattered — and a little touched — to think that of all the sordid hotel rooms you must have been in, you should have remembered that one. *(Drinks.)*

IRENE.   Bayard is not dead!

HARRY.   Who?

IRENE.   The Chevalier Bayard!

HARRY.   Oh?

IRENE.   Somewhere in that funny, music hall soul of yours is the spirit of Leander and Abelard and Galahad. You give up everything — you risk your life — you have walked unafraid into the valley of the shadow — to aid and comfort a damsel in distress. Isn't that the truth?

HARRY.   Yeah — that's the truth — simply and plainly put. Now, listen to me, babe, when are you going to break down and tell me who the hell are you?

IRENE.   Does it matter so very much who I am?

HARRY.   No, no. I like you like you are.

IRENE.   Give me some more champagne. *(Harry crosses L. to her and pours some more in her glass, then empties bottle in his, and drinks. Irene drops her Russian accent.)* I am not a Romanoff — far from it. I just like to see the light in people's eyes when I tell them I am a Russian princess. They are all such snobs. I am not going to tell the truth to them, why should I? — Their whole life is a lie. But I can tell the truth to you because you are an honest man.

HARRY.   *(Draws himself up proudly.)* Oh, I am, am I? *(Crosses L. to bar, bottle in hand. Irene drains her glass.)* Another bottle of champagne! *(Opens bar door.)*

CAPTAIN.   *(In bar.)* Mr. Van?

HARRY.   Hi, Captain! *(Puts empty bottle of champagne on bar.)*

CAPTAIN.   *(In bar.)* What happened? Did you miss the train?

HARRY.   No. I didn't miss the train — just a goddamned fool! *(Closes bar door. Irene has come D. from platform, holding her empty glass, stands at R. end of bend of piano. Harry crosses R. to her. She kisses him.)*

IRENE.   I love you, Harry.

HARRY.   You do, eh?

IRENE.   Yes, ever since that night in the Governor Bryan Hotel I have loved you. You have a heart that I can trust. And whatever I say to you I know it will never be misunderstood.

HARRY.   Yeah! I had you tagged from the start.

IRENE. And you adore me too, don't you, darling?

HARRY. No, I told you once, no.

IRENE. *(Puts arms around his neck.)* No, you mustn't admit it.

HARRY. And quit pawing me, will you? And we don't want any misunderstanding, do we?

IRENE. Oh, dear, no!

HARRY. If you're going to hook up with me, it's only for professional reasons — see?

IRENE. I see.

HARRY. And I'm the manager.

IRENE. Oh, yes.

HARRY. I'll fix it with the Captain to get across the border tomorrow or the next day. We'll join the girls in Geneva — that's as good a place as any to rehearse the Code.

IRENE. The Code! No, you must tell it to me at once.

HARRY. At once! It's a very deep, complicated, scientific problem.

IRENE. I shall be able to do that very easily. *(Crosses R. to C.)*

HARRY. Say, listen, if you're unusually smart and apply yourself, you'll get a fairly good idea of it after six months of study and rehearsal. *(Auguste enters from bar L. with bottle of champagne, crosses R. below Harry, refills Irene's glass, crosses L., gives Harry the bottle on "lay off liquor," and exits into bar.)*

IRENE. A mind reader! You're right. I shall be able to do that very well!

HARRY. And another thing, if you're going to qualify for this act with me, you'll have to lay off liquor. I mean, after we finish this one. *(Pours some in his glass.)* It's a well-known fact that booze and science don't mix. *(Drains his glass.)*

IRENE. *(As one in a trance, lapses into Russian accent.)* I don't think I shall use my own name —

HARRY. No?

IRENE. No. I shall call myself — Namoura ... Namoura the Great — assisted by Harry Van. *(Drains her glass. Harry, nonplused at her colossal nerve, is speechless. Comes D. to above table D.L.)* I shall wear black velvet — cut very plain — you know, with my skin, ivory white. I must have something to hold. One white flower, hah? No — a little white prayer book — *(Warning*

95

air raid siren is heard off U.R. She throws her glass down on floor. Harry puts champagne bottle on table D.L., goes to L. of Irene. Captain, Major and Auguste rush out of bar. Captain rushes across below Harry and Irene to window. Major rushes U.C. and exits L. Auguste rushes for window. Pittaluga enters from L. and U.C. at same time, and comes D.)

CAPTAIN. *(As he comes rushing out.)* Signor Maggiori andate a la caserma e date l'alarme del gas!

MAJOR. *Venga lei anche!*

HARRY. What's up, Captain?

PITTALUGA. *(To Auguste.) Auguste! Chiude le persiane … Fa presto, presto! (Rushes out U.C. and R. Auguste begins to let Venetian blinds down. Airplane motors overhead are now heard coming nearer.)*

CAPTAIN. *(Looks up through window and turns to Irene and Harry.)* French aeroplanes. It is reprisal for last night. They are coming to destroy our base here. They have no right to attack this hotel. But — there may easily be an accident. I advise the cellar. *(Quickly crosses L. above them to arch C.)*

IRENE. Oh, no, no, no.

CAPTAIN. I entreat you, Madame, not to be reckless. I have enough on my conscience now, without adding to it your innocent life!

IRENE. Don't worry, Captain!

CAPTAIN. God be with you, Madame! *(Rushes out U.C. and L.)*

IRENE. We're in the war, Harry. *(Auguste has put down three Venetian blinds and rushes across L. above Harry and Irene, U.C., exits L.)*

HARRY. Yeah. What are we going to do? Go out and say "boo"?

IRENE. Sing to them!

HARRY. My voice don't feel appropriate. Too bad we can't get Chaliapin. *(Signor and Signora Rossi rush across at back from R. to L., followed by Pittaluga.)*

PITTALUGA. *(In arch C.)* Everyone goes into the cellar. Quick! It is dangerous here!

IRENE. Ridiculous!

HARRY. Thanks very much, Signor.

PITTALUGA. You have been warned! *(Rushes out C. and to L.)*

96

IRENE.   Here we are, on the top of the world — and he wants us to go in the cellar! Do you want to go in the cellar?

HARRY.   Do you?

IRENE.   No. If a bomb comes, it is worse in the cellar.

HARRY.   All right, babe, I'll stick by you. *(Bomb burst quite near, and room is plunged into darkness. Weird flares of light off windows at R.)*

IRENE.   *(Rushes R. to windows.)* Come and watch it, Harry, come and watch it. *(She peers through slats of blind.)* Oh, it is superb! *(Harry has crossed R. to her at window.)* It is positively Wagnerian!

HARRY.   It looks to me exactly like "Hell's Angels." *(Another bomb explosion, followed by a flare and a burst of machine gun fire. Harry grabs Irene by hand and rushes L. across stage to piano. Lights his cigarette lighter to give light to darkened room, puts it on keyboard of piano. As he lights lighter, the spots in piano and in L. wall come up and flicker to simulate the light from lighter. Harry sits at piano and begins playing "The Ride of the Walkyries."* Irene stands R. of him on platform.)* I used to play the piano in picture theatres!

IRENE.   I hate those films.

HARRY.   I don't. I love 'em. I love every one of them. *(From time the first bomb has burst there is a constant roar of plane motors and distant cannonading.)*

IRENE.   Do you realize — the whole world has gone to war? The *whole world!*

HARRY.   Yeah. I realize it. But don't ask me why. Because I've stopped trying to figure it out.

IRENE.   I know why. It is just to kill us — you and me. *(Bomb burst very close, Harry stops playing.)* Because we are the little people and for us the deadliest weapons are the most merciful ... *(Another bomb bursts close by. Harry starts playing "Onward, Christian Soldiers." Both begin singing.)*

BOTH.

"Onward, Christian Soldiers,
Marching as to war —"

CURTAIN

* See Special Note on Songs and Recordings on copyright page.

PROPERTY LIST

Cigarette cases (CAPTAIN, HARRY, CHERRY)
Cigarettes (CAPTAIN, HARRY, CHERRY, IRENE)
Lighters/matches (CAPTAIN, DOCTOR, HARRY, DON,
    CHERRY)
Cigars (DOCTOR, WEBER)
Book (DOCTOR)
Brandy and soda (AUGUSTE)
Suitcases (DUMPSTY)
Notebook and pencil (CAPTAIN)
Briefcase (HARRY)
7 passports (HARRY)
French magazine (QUILLERY)
Silver snuff box (HARRY)
Glass of mineral water (DUMPSTY, AUGUSTE)
Coins (DOCTOR, CHERRY, ELAINE)
Drinks (DUMPSTY)
Chewing gum (HARRY)
Tray (DUMPSTY)
Cocktails (AUGUSTE)
Italian newspaper (QUILLERY)
Tray (DUMPSTY) with:
    glass of vodka
    waiter's check
    small pencil
Bottle of vodka (DUMPSTY) with:
    3 glasses
Glass of brandy (WEBER)
Leather cigar case (WEBER) with:
    cigar
    cutter
    lighter/matches
Coffee and liqueur (AUGUSTE)
3 buckets with champagne bottles (DUMPSTY)
Tray with 9 glasses (DUMPSTY)
Sewing box and black silk stockings (SHIRLEY)
Small mirror and tweezers (BEBE)

Portable writing portfolio (EDNA)
Cards (BEULAH)
Briefcase (CAPTAIN) with:
    papers
    passports
Bundled books and umbrella (DOCTOR)
Eyeglass case with eyeglasses (DOCTOR)
Envelope of money (WEBER)
Note of money (IRENE)

SOUND EFFECTS

4-piece orchestra music
Warning sirens
Handbells
Airplane motors
Airplanes
Bombs
Flare
Machine gunfire
Distant cannonading

NEW PLAYS

- **SMASH by Jeffrey Hatcher.** Based on the novel, AN UNSOCIAL SOCIALIST by George Bernard Shaw, the story centers on a millionaire Socialist who leaves his bride on their wedding day because he fears his passion for her will get in the way of his plans to overthrow the British government. *"SMASH is witty, cunning, intelligent, and skillful."* –*Seattle Weekly*. *"SMASH is a wonderfully high-style British comedy of manners that evokes the world of Shaw's high-minded heroes and heroines, but shaped by a post modern sensibility."* –*Seattle Herald*. [5M, 5W] ISBN: 0-8222-1553-5

- **PRIVATE EYES by Steven Dietz.** A comedy of suspicion in which nothing is ever quite what it seems. *"Steven Dietz's ... Pirandellian smooch to the mercurial nature of theatrical illusion and romantic truth, Dietz's spiraling structure and breathless pacing provide enough of an oxygen rush to revive any moribund audience member ... Dietz's mastery of playmaking ... is cause for kudos."* –*The Village Voice*. *"The cleverest and most artful piece presented at the 21st annual [Humana] festival was PRIVATE EYES by writer-director Steven Dietz."* –*The Chicago Tribune*. [3M, 2W] ISBN: 0-8222-1619-1

- **DIMLY PERCEIVED THREATS TO THE SYSTEM by Jon Klein.** Reality and fantasy overlap with hilarious results as this unforgettable family attempts to survive the nineties. *"Here's a play whose point about fractured families goes to the heart, mind -- and ears."* –*The Washington Post*. *" ... an end-of-the millennium comedy about a family on the verge of a nervous breakdown ... Trenchant and hilarious ... "* –*The Baltimore Sun*. [2M, 4W] ISBN: 0-8222-1677-9

- **HONOUR by Joanna Murray-Smith.** In a series of intense confrontations, a wife, husband, lover and daughter negotiate the forces of passion, lust, history, responsibility and honour. *"Tight, crackling dialogue (usually played out in punchy verbal duels) captures characters unable to deal with emotions ... Murray-Smith effectively places her characters in situations that strip away pretense."* –*Variety*. *"HONOUR might just capture a few honors of its own."* –*Time Out Magazine*. [1M, 3W] ISBN: 0-8222-1683-3

- **NINE ARMENIANS by Leslie Ayvazian.** A revealing portrait of three generations of an Armenian-American family. *" ... Ayvazian's obvious personal exploration ... is evocative, and her picture of an American Life colored nostalgically by an increasingly alien ethnic tradition, is persuasively embedded into a script of a certain supple grace ... "* –*The NY Post*. *"... NINE ARMENIANS is a warm, likable work that benefits from ... Ayvazian's clear-headed insight into the dynamics of a close-knit family ... "* –*Variety*. [5M, 5W] ISBN: 0-8222-1602-7

- **PSYCHOPATHIA SEXUALIS by John Patrick Shanley.** Fetishes and psychiatry abound in this scathing comedy about a man and his father's argyle socks. *"John Patrick Shanley's new play, PSYCHOPATHIA SEXUALIS is ... perfectly poised between daffy comedy and believable human neurosis which Shanley combines so well ... "* –*The LA Times*. *"John Patrick Shanley's PSYCHOPATHIA SEXUALIS is a salty boulevard comedy with a bittersweet theme ... "* –*New York Magazine*. *"A tour de force of witty, barbed dialogue."* –*Variety*. [3M, 2W] ISBN: 0-8222-1615-9

DRAMATISTS PLAY SERVICE, INC.
440 Park Avenue South, New York, NY 10016 212-683-8960 Fax 212-213-1539
postmaster@dramatists.com www.dramatists.com

NEW PLAYS

• **A QUESTION OF MERCY by David Rabe.** The Obie Award-winning playwright probes the sensitive and controversial issue of doctor-assisted suicide in the age of AIDS in this poignant drama. *"There are many devastating ironies in Mr. Rabe's beautifully considered, piercingly clear-eyed work ... " –The NY Times. "With unsettling candor and disturbing insight, the play arouses pity and understanding of a troubling subject ... Rabe's provocative tale is an affirmation of dignity that rings clear and true." –Variety.* [6M, 1W] ISBN: 0-8222-1643-4

• **A DOLL'S HOUSE by Henrik Ibsen, adapted by Frank McGuinness. Winner of the 1997 Tony Award for best revival.** *"New, raw, gut-twisting and gripping. Easily the hottest drama this season." –USA Today. "Bold, brilliant and alive." –The Wall Street Journal. "A thunderclap of an evening that takes your breath away." –Time. "The stuff of Broadway legend." –Associated Press.* [4M, 4W, 2 boys] ISBN: 0-8222-1636-1

• **THE WAITING ROOM by Lisa Loomer.** Three women from different centuries meet in a doctor's waiting room in this dark comedy about the timeless quest for beauty -- and its cost. *" ... THE WAITING ROOM ... is a bold, risky melange of conflicting elements that is ... terrifically moving ... There's no resisting the fierce emotional pull of the play." – The NY Times. " ... one of the high points of this year's Off-Broadway season ... THE WAITING ROOM is well worth a visit." –Back Stage.* [7M, 4W, flexible casting] ISBN: 0-8222-1594-2

• **MR. PETERS' CONNECTIONS by Arthur Miller.** Mr. Miller describes the protagonist as existing in a dream-like state when the mind is "freed to roam from real memories to conjectures, from trivialities to tragic insights, from terror of death to glorying in one's being alive." With this memory play, the Tony Award and Pulitzer Prize-winner reaffirms his stature as the world's foremost dramatist. *" ... a cross between Joycean stream-of-consciousness and Strindberg's dream plays, sweetened with a dose of William Saroyan's philosophical whimsy ... CONNECTIONS is most intriguing ... Miller scholars will surely find many connections of their own to make between this work and the author's earlier plays." –The NY Times.* [5M, 3W] ISBN: 0-8222-1687-6

• **THE STEWARD OF CHRISTENDOM by Sebastian Barry.** A freely imagined portrait of the author's great-grandfather, the last Chief Superintendent of the Dublin Metropolitan Police. *"MAGNIFICENT ... the cool, elegiac eye of James Joyce's THE DEAD; the bleak absurdity of Samuel Beckett's lost, primal characters; the cosmic anger of KING LEAR ... " –The NY Times. "Sebastian Barry's compassionate imaging of an ancestor he never knew is among the most poignant onstage displays of humanity in recent memory." –Variety.* [5M, 4W] ISBN: 0-8222-1609-4

• **SYMPATHETIC MAGIC by Lanford Wilson. Winner of the 1997 Obie for best play.** The mysteries of the universe, and of human and artistic creation, are explored in this award-winning play. *"Lanford Wilson's idiosyncratic SYMPATHETIC MAGIC is his BEST PLAY YET ... the rare play you WANT ... chock-full of ideas, incidents, witty or poetic lines, scientific and philosophical argument ... you'll find your intellectual faculties racing." – New York Magazine. "The script is like a fully notated score, next to which most new plays are cursory lead sheets." –The Village Voice.* [5M, 3W] ISBN: 0-8222-1630-2

DRAMATISTS PLAY SERVICE, INC.
440 Park Avenue South, New York, NY 10016 212-683-8960 Fax 212-213-1539
postmaster@dramatists.com www.dramatists.com